Split Rock Wildway

Split Rock Wildway:
Scouting the Adirondack Park's
Most Diverse Wildlife Corridor

John Davis

Essex Editions

Published in the United States by Essex Editions.
ISBN-10:0-9967870-7-0
ISBN-13:978-0-9967870-7-9

Library of Congress Control Number: 2017953142

Essex Editions
Post Office Box 25
Essex, New York 12936
www.essexeditions.com
contact@essexeditions.com

This book is dedicated to the creatures and places introduced herein. Family and friends have made its production possible, but the aim of this little publication is to inspire ourselves and fellow Adirondack residents and visitors to more fully appreciate and protect the wildlife of our beloved homeland. To the carnivores who prowl our forests, to the fish who swim the lakes and rivers, to the birds who fly overhead, to the trees that provide homes for all. . . I offer the following words of praise.

Contents

Section I:
Big and Toothy Animals

Section 2:
Slithering, Crawling, and Hopping Things

Section 3:
Winged Ones

Section 4:
Finned Neighbors

Section 5:
Not So Easy Being Green

Foreword

In the summer of 2003 I saw a timber rattlesnake for the first time. The snake was slow-moving, nearly black, thick as a late summer zucchini, and spanning a remarkably wide portion of Lakeshore Road's northbound lane. It was more intent on basking than crossing from Split Rock Wild Forest to Webb Royce Swamp, and it exhibited no sign of aggression despite my proximity.

A couple of hours later I returned and discovered the same rattlesnake lifeless, crushed by a vehicle.

The high I had been riding since my earlier encounter crashed. Wonder and excitement were eclipsed by heartbreak. Guilt swept over me. Could I safely have relocated the snake to the far side of the road? What if I had simply waited until the rattler made it to safety, my hazard lights flashing to warn oncoming cars to slow down? Might this majestic creature have survived?

◆ ◆ ◆

Some years later when the Essex on Lake Champlain community blog was launched to celebrate the rich heritage of Essex, New York, and environs I turned to close friend and frequent conservation coconspirator John Davis with a challenge. Would he consider writing a series of articles about local wildlife? Perhaps investigating the relevance of rattlesnakes (and other native creatures) might increase public interest and respect and – possibly, *hopefully* – might even decrease accidental and/or unnecessary bloodshed.

I was 100% confident that, should he accept the challenge, we would all profit immeasurably from his knowledge and passion. John has inspired and educated me for a decade and a half. His humility and reverence for the natural world; his firsthand

I

experience as a learned, enthusiastic, and athletic wildways scout; his uncanny knack for bridging juxtaposed factions; and his linguistic (dare I say lyric?) virtuosity repeatedly and consistently sets the gold standard.

John agreed to research and write the wildlife series, sagely focusing the project on Split Rock Wildway. Over the next three years he published a parade of popular posts reverently illuminating many of the wild neighbors with whom we share this liminal Eden between the Adirondack High Peaks and Lake Champlain. Though lighthearted and accessible, John's writing never veered from the importance of better understanding, better respecting, and better protecting our wildway and its diverse inhabitants (both permanent and passers-through). From his first posts about cougars, John's perspective resonated with a broad audience, sowing the seeds for reworking and augmenting the series into a book.

I am profoundly grateful to John Davis for transforming possibility into reality. Again.

Bountiful thanks are also due the Eddy Foundation for underwriting publication; Bill Amadon, Sheri Amsel, Steven Kellogg, Rod MacIver, Kevin Raines, Larry Barns, and Larry Master for contributing enchanting artwork; Chris Maron and Matt Foley for developing the map; and Katie Shepard for expert editing and project management. Bravo!

G^{eo} *Davis*
Autumn 2017

THE
SPLIT
ROCK
WILDWAY

W
S — ⊕ — N
E

☆ Wadhams

Split Rock Wildway

Split Rock Wildway

☆ Whallonsburg

Lake Champlain

Split
Rock

Steven Kellogg

Introduction

SPLIT ROCK WILDWAY

The Most Diverse Wildlife Corridor in the Largest Park in the Richest State in the Most Powerful Nation in the History of Life on Earth!

A mother black bear with cubs waking from winter hibernation beneath a snow-covered spruce/fir thicket in the Adirondack Mountains of northern New York may serve her family well by leading them down and east toward the fertile, equable Champlain Valley on the west coast of the Northeast's longest lake and the eastern edge of the East's largest park. She will be wise to find a safe sunny spot for her cubs to nap while she climbs the tallest nearby tree to scout a broadly forested route from the cold snowy mountains down to the valley, where wetlands are already mostly melted and plants are putting out new growth.

If the big yellow birch that Mama Bear climbs has the right vantage point, she may choose a path from the High Peaks easterly through smaller mountains to the North Branch of the Boquet River. She may then lead her cubs downriver to one of the few relatively safe crossings on Interstate 87, the river's span here under the highway being broad and free of houses. If she gets her family safely past I-87, they can continue east into the fertile West Champlain Hills. She may choose a safe course to the saddle-like pair of glade-rich hills known as Boquet Mountain, then southeast to the oaky, bumpy ridge called Coon Mountain, then east again to the wildest part of Lake Champlain's lengthy shoreline, Split Rock Wild Forest. Mother bear and cubs will thus have traversed Split Rock Wildway — a critical wildlife corridor linking the highly productive (for wildlife and people) Champlain Valley with the rugged High Peaks to the west.

Black bears climb trees for food, often beechnuts or acorns, and shelter. © Sheri Amsel, www.exploringnature.org

The subtitle above may flirt with hyperbole, but Split Rock Wildway and the much larger Adirondack Park of which it is a part are in fact bold, monumental efforts toward reconnecting wild habitats and stabilizing climate. The ten or more conservation and recreation groups helping protect Split Rock Wildway are working for wildlife, quiet recreation, and a safe climate, within the context of a world-class park and an internationally acclaimed Biosphere Reserve.

Local and regional conservationists are also working for safe food and vibrant economies. Indeed, we envision the peaceful coexistence of small towns and abundant wildlife. On both the New York and Vermont sides of the lake, the Champlain Valley is enjoying a revival of organic and family farms. Increasingly evident in the Adirondack's Champlain Valley, small-scale farming is seen as complementary to wildlands preservation and integral to achieving sustainable natural and human communities.

Getting to Know Our Neighbors

The book you are now reading is essentially a scout's report on neighbors met during rambles through Split Rock Wildway. In writing, editing, and designing this book, George Davis, Katie Shepard, and I – along with our artist friends who generously donated works – offer a friendly, wandering look at some of the wild animals and plants who share our eastern Adirondack home with us. My collection of Split Rock Wildway accounts is not intended as a technical field guide or scientific treatise, though it is informed by natural history, ecology, and conservation biology.

Most of this book is adapted from a series of wildlife blog posts that I originally wrote for the vibrant community blog Essex on Lake Champlain (essexonlakechamplain.com). With encouragement from editors George Davis and Katie Shepard, I continue to bring the outdoors online for residents and visitors to our enchanting edge of Adirondack Park. I encourage you to read these periodic posts, and I invite you to submit your own observations and encounters with our wild neighbors. As we explore more of Split Rock Wildway, and write and receive more stories, we will craft a companion to this little book.

Regarding my authorship, I would like to add a brief caveat. I aspire to become a good naturalist, but I am not a degreed biologist. I tag along with biologists in the field every chance that I get, and that is how I have learned most of my natural history. The wildlife accounts in this book are based on my rambles through Split Rock Wildway, my persistent questioning of biologist friends, and my studies of field guides. Any biological mistakes in this book are my own, not my guides' or my editors'. Please, readers, let us know of any mistakes you find or any observations you make that contradict my claims.

We hope that this book will inspire greater appreciation and understanding of the many other species with whom we share our hilly and watery home. Meanwhile, back to that wandering bear family, and a little more on the ground they will tread.

Where the Bears Wander

Fortunately for the bears, birds, and trout, geology has afforded habitat connections from the High Peaks to Lake Champlain. Among such critical natural links are rivers, particularly the Boquet, AuSable, and Saranac, and a section of the West Champlain Hills that conservationists know as Split Rock Wildway. This wildlife corridor runs southwest through the Split Rock Range on Lake Champlain, west over Coon Mountain, northwest over Sprig and Cob Hills and Boquet Mountain, then west to the Jay Range and the High Peaks. It runs from habitat of lake sturgeon, river otter, and bald eagle to that of stunted spruce, American marten, and Bicknell's thrush, with brook trout plying the waters between, and our bruin friends moving up and down on land and by water with the seasons.

Split Rock Wild Forest anchors the Wildway on the east; Jay Mountain Wilderness anchors it on the west. Related habitat connections extend southward through the Westport Woods (partially protected by a state-held conservation easement), stretching almost to Port Henry; and north (less continuously) over other West Champlain Hills, such as Rattlesnake, Sugarloaf, and Skagerack; and west of there to Poke-O-Moonshine (with its towering cliffs and profusion of tree species).

Split Rock Wildway roughly corresponds to an arm of mountain bedrock, anorthosite, reaching from the High Peaks through the

Champlain Valley in a wide band of rocky hills. Historically, this swath (shaped roughly like a swoosh) of rugged ground remained largely forested, while fertile valley soils to the north and south were converted to agriculture. Split Rock Wildway also includes a branch of forested habitat reaching southwest from Split Rock Wild Forest past Westport and westward through the Westport Woods and on into the mountains.

All this is set within New York's Adirondack Park, which at 6 million acres in size is the largest park in the Lower 48 United States. It is an unusual park, though, in that it is more than half private land. About 2.8 of the 6 million acres are state-owned Forest Preserve, guaranteed "Forever Wild" protection by the New York State Constitution: some of the strongest land protection in the world. Roughly 1.1 million of those 2.8 million acres are given the additional layer of Wilderness protection. Adirondack Park is set within the even larger Champlain-Adirondack Biosphere Reserve, an honorary (not regulatory) designation bestowed upon the Champlain Valley in both New York and Vermont and extending up the east and west sides of the Adirondack and Green Mountains, respectively. It adds up to more than 9 million acres, making it one of the largest Biosphere Reserves in the world.

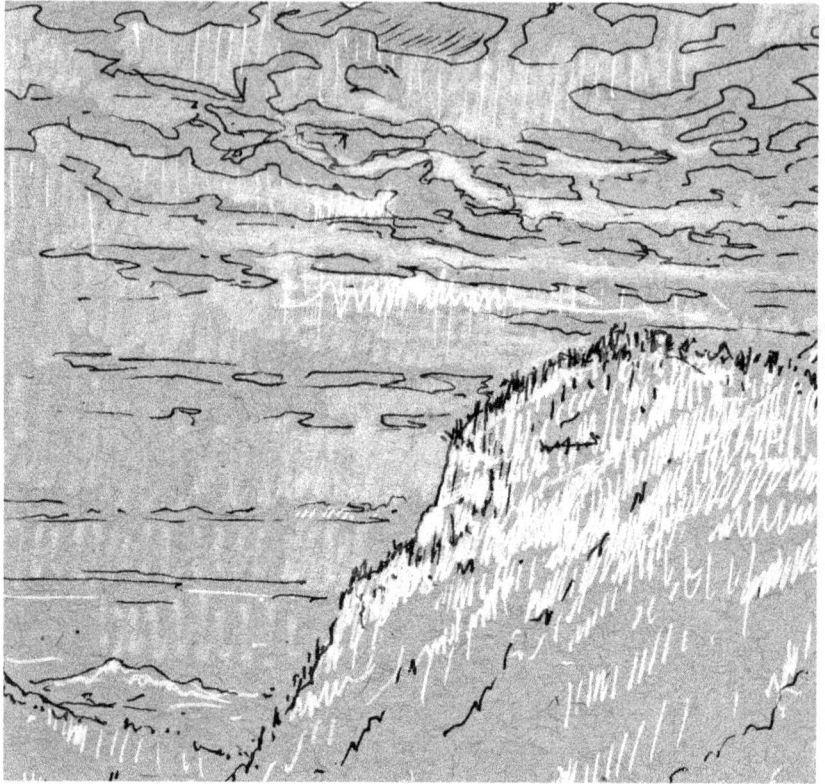

Raven Pass, here seen from Route 9N between Westport and Elizabethtown, would help link Split Rock Wildway with forest blocks to the south, but the major roads in this area need safe wildlife crossings. © Kevin Raines

Protecting Both Public and Private Lands

Habitat connections (or wildways or wildlife corridors or linkages) within Adirondack Park and between the Park and outside wildlands have been recognized by Wildlands Network, The Rewilding Institute, Keeping Track, Wildlife Conservation Society, Adirondack Council, Adirondack Nature Conservancy & Land Trust, Northeast Wilderness Trust, Open Space Institute, Eddy Foundation, Two Countries One Forest, Adirondack Wild, Protect the Adirondacks, Champlain Area Trails, Lake Champlain

Land Trust, and other conservation groups as regionally important. Public lands conservation is necessary but not sufficient to protect these biological connections. Equally important are incentives for private landowners to protect their lands and wildlife thereon.

Thankfully for outdoor recreationists as well as wildlife, we are blessed in Adirondack Park with expansive public lands. Indeed, the biggest conservation landowner in Split Rock Wildway is the New York Department of Environmental Conservation. NYDEC owns nearly 4000 acres in Split Rock Wildway, among its 2.8 million across the Park, plus another half million throughout the state (the second-biggest complex being in the Catskills), giving it the potential to become a player of national significance in wildlife corridor protection and in carbon sequestration.

The DEC also holds conservation easements on more than 700,000 acres of privately owned lands across Adirondack Park. Though widely recognized as an urgent need, private lands conservation may not proceed much farther without better incentives for landowners to be good stewards. An impetus for conservation groups exploring the possibility of selling carbon credits is (together with finding an income source to help cover stewardship costs) to further programs that would reward landowners for doing the right thing: pay them to leave their trees standing and their lands intact. If our country finally has the good sense to put a price on carbon, land trusts, and other conservation-minded landowners should be able to sell the value of the carbon they are sequestering in the ground by allowing trees to grow and forests to grow old. (Old forests store more carbon than do young forests.)

Biological Riches

Jerry Jenkins, author of the *Adirondack Atlas, Climate Change in the Adirondacks*, and the upcoming *Northern Forest Atlas* series, showed in his plant associations reports for Wildlife Conservation Society and Adirondack Nature Conservancy that the West Champlain Hills are botanically one of the richest areas in the Northeast, rare in this region for their dry yet rich oak/hickory/hophornbeam community. Jerry has catalogued dozens of fertility indicators and xeric specialists here that are rare or absent elsewhere in the Park, including white and chestnut oaks, stiff sandwort, rafinesque viburnum, Douglas knotweed, bristly gooseberry, leatherwood, and woodland sunflower.

The West Champlain Hills are also rich in animals, and Split Rock Wildway is home or movement habitat for many shy, sensitive, or wide-ranging species. Among focal species seen here (many of which Keeping Track has formally documented) are black bear, bobcat, coyote, ermine, long-tailed weasel, mink, fisher, river otter, red and gray foxes, moose, peregrine falcon, osprey, bald eagle, wood duck, hooded merganser, great blue and green herons, timber rattlesnake, map turtle, spotted salamander, and at least seven frog and toad species.

The great water off Split Rock Wildway, between the Adirondack and Green Mountains, Lake Champlain, is itself worthy of top conservation attention. Historically, Lake Champlain supported populations of American eel, landlocked Atlantic salmon, lake sturgeon, lake trout, brook trout, sauger, brook lamprey, and even harbor seal. The seal and several of these fish have been eliminated or greatly reduced by past overexploitation and dams on lake tributaries. Some of the same groups leading land protection efforts in Split Rock Wildway are also advancing the related needs of aquatic species, which will greatly benefit from forest protection but also need removal of man-made dams and exotic species.

Half Way Home

Protection of Split Rock Wildway is nearly half complete. For the long-term viability of the wildlife corridor, at least 15,000 continuous acres from Split Rock to the Jay Range need protection. So far, the state, Eddy Foundation, Open Space Institute, Adirondack Land Trust, Northeast Wilderness Trust, Champlain Area Trails, and conservation-minded families have collectively conserved about 7,000 acres. Needed steps now include:

- NYDEC and land trusts should acquire strong conservation easements – or full ownership if available – on major holdings in the area;

- create a revolving loan fund or land acquisition endowment, to secure critical properties that go on the market, including any sizable lands around Coon and Boquet Mountains;

- restore missing or diminished species, as explored in this book;

- foster *farming with the wild* principles (wildfarmalliance.org, essexfarminstitute.org) and ecological forestry standards (protectadks.org, us.fsc.org) for worked lands in the area; and

- complete the footpath system that will link local villages and enhance the recreational economy. Champlain Area Trails (champlainareatrails.com) has lately at least tripled trail mileage in the Wildway – carefully routing paths so as to afford hikers and skiers scenic views but not disturb sensitive habitat – and has in place most of a trail linking Westport and Essex.

The biggest remaining challenges are creating financial and other incentives to reward wildlife-friendly land-stewardship, and encouraging coexistence between people and our wild neighbors.

While property tax reform (to extract taxes from harmful practices, not from landownership) is a top priority, the best near-term hope for conservation landowners may be selling carbon credits for protecting wild forests. Beneficiaries will be natural and human communities for this and future generations, including that Mama Bear's great grand-cubs and those of our children lucky enough to see them.

Section I:

Big and Toothy Animals

Though popularly known as 'mountain lion', the cougar, or puma or panther, actually is more closely related to the cheetah than to the lion and can thrive in most American habitats — if not persecuted. © Larry Master, www.masterimages.org

Split Rock Wildway not only links Lake Champlain with the Adirondack Mountains, it links the St. Lawrence/Champlain Ecoregion with the Northern Appalachian/Acadian Ecoregion. Spanning ecozones, Split Rock Wildway enjoys a wide diversity of wildlife species. We've lost some of our biggest animals and trees, unfortunately, but thanks to conservation measures, many species are actually faring better today than they were a century ago.

Early human hunters are thought to have overhunted into extinction the Pleistocene mega-fauna that until 12,000 or so years ago roamed much of our continent. The loss of mammoths, giant ground sloths, saber-toothed cats, dire wolves, and dozens of other large mammals thousands of years ago greatly diminished North America's grandeur. More recently, the felling of the eastern deciduous and northern transition forests, along with the regional extirpation of several of the carnivores who survived the Pleistocene overkill – cougars, lynx, gray wolves, and wolverines – further diminished our lands and waters. These extirpated but not extinct carnivores can and should be restored, as we'll discuss in this book.

Still gracing our lands and waters, though, are such charismatic mammals as black bear, bobcat, coyote, red fox, fisher, river otter, mink, moose, and white-tail deer. If this book does its job, it will strengthen support both for conservation of the beautiful animals still here and restoration of the species we unkindly eliminated in the past.

Chapter I:
Carnivores and Public Health
Fear of Carnivores Misplaced

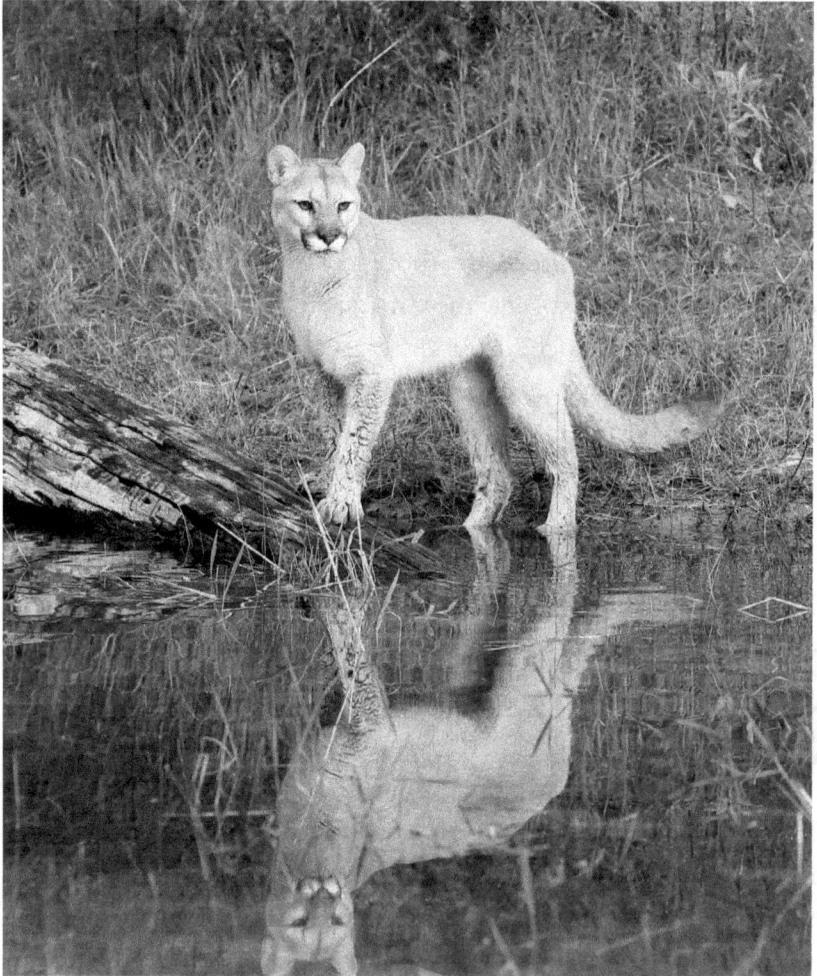

The rare cougar who somehow miraculously disperses to the East from the West likely does so largely by following waterways, which offer cover and prey in riparian forests. © Larry Master, www.masterimages.org

If ever there was a time in American history when we had reason to fear being eaten by bigger animals, it is past. The greatest dangers in our lives these days are self-imposed: fast cars, fast food, pollution, climate chaos...

All the wild carnivores in North America combined do not kill as many people as do domestic dogs. Cars kill thousands of times as many people as do animals. The animal that kills the most people in the United States now is deer — our elimination of native predators having allowed prey numbers to soar past natural levels, resulting in countless, sometimes fatal, collisions between cars and wildlife.

Bobcats, cougars, and either red or gray wolves or both belong in the Adirondacks and Northern Appalachians, and they would be regulating deer herds, if present in ample numbers. The importance of native predators is not just in the deer they actually cull from the herd — usually the weaker ones, whereas human hunters often go against natural selection by targeting the trophy animals — it's also in how they keep the ungulates wary and moving, preventing over-browsing of wildflowers, white-cedars, and other preferred vegetation.

John Laundre, author of *Phantoms of the Prairie: The Return of the Cougar to the Midwest,* and other biologists have used the term "ecology of fear" to stress the importance of top predators for behavioral changes. Absent their hunters, grazers and browsers get chubby and complacent as they munch down the forest.

As a wildways scout, I've been fortunate to trek thousands of miles in recent years in many of the wildest parts of the East, including Adirondack Wilderness Areas, and in the West, especially along the Rocky Mountains. I've seen most of North America's native carnivores — always in positive, life-affirming experiences – but so far, I've seen cougars only as tracks, scrapes, and carrion. Cougars are so elusive, you can live decades near them and never even glimpse one.

Cougar Rewilding Foundation, Wildlands Network, and The Rewilding Institute are among the groups calling for their return to the Adirondacks and Northern Appalachians We are fortunate to have in the Adirondacks enough wild country and prey (deer especially, but also beaver, snowshoe hare, and other smaller animals) to support cougar recovery.

Welcoming Home Missing Species

Many local residents insist the "big cats" – cougars, pumas, panthers, mountain lions, catamounts (multiple names for the same animal) – are already here, or were never fully eradicated. From my readings and observations, it seems the many reported sightings of cougars usually fall into several confusing categories:

* People excitedly thinking they're seeing cougars when actually they are seeing the great cat's smaller distant cousin, the bobcat, or even a golden retriever or deer or another big tawny mammal.

* Released or escaped pet cougars, for some people don't care what the laws say about holding wild animals captive.

* Widely dispersing cougars, usually young males, leaving areas far to the west where they are being shot and trapped and following forested connections eastward, but not finding mates, and eventually being shot or hit by cars in their search for new territories.

From my ramblings and readings, I fear we do not now have breeding populations of cougars in the East north of the remnant population in South Florida.

I believe that we have many reasons to help cougars return home safely, not least of which is the sheer thrill of glimpsing a big wild cat disappearing into a big wild forest.

More scientifically than my field reporting, the Cougar Rewilding Foundation has done expansive research and concluded that we do not now have, but would greatly benefit from, a functioning population of cougars in our Appalachian and Adirondack forests. CRF biologist John Laundre has also concluded that Adirondack Park has ample habitat and prey for a viable cougar population.

If welcomed back to our region, cougars would cull out the weaker members of the deer herd, plus eat smaller prey animals like porcupine and beaver. © Sheri Amsel, www.exploringnature.org

Our woods and our lives will be safer if we allow cougars and other missing predators to return. While the likelihood of being eaten by a big wild toothy animal is vanishingly remote (vending machines and rotten fruit, for a couple of examples, kill more people than do native carnivores), the likelihood of being sickened by Lyme disease or another emerging public health threat associated with fragmented ecosystems is significant. Cougars and other predators hold in check numbers of the smaller animals that carry such pathogens as the bacterium that causes Lyme disease.

Intact, connected forests, extensive enough to house full suites of native predators, are healthier not just for wildlife but also for people in nearby towns. For evidence, take a long walk in the woods, starting in a badly logged woodlot then making your way to a big piece of Forest Preserve, resting occasionally along the way to read from Richard Ostfelt's book *Lyme Disease: Ecology of a Complex System* or Cristina Eisenberg's *The Wolf's Tooth* or Jim Estes and John Terborgh's *Trophic Cascades*. Or follow Keeping Track founder Sue Morse on the paths of our area's four-legged wanderers.

For New York's Adirondack Park to be indisputably the wildest, healthiest landscape in the East, we need to welcome home cougars and wolves. We should also study the viability of restoring lynx to the Park, and research whether wolverine were present here. Lynx depend heavily on snowshoe hare for prey, and do best in cold snowy environments (as do wolverines); so they may prove susceptible to warming climate. Still, snowshoe hare thus far seem to be surviving warming weather just fine, so perhaps lynx could too. A successful restoration of lynx could give our communities the confidence to welcome home cougars next. Then should come wolves...

Wolves are the consummate top predator in North America, serving as rangers or guardians of wild ecosystems by keeping herbivores from severely over-browsing or overgrazing plant communities. Wolves help keep white-tail and mule deer, moose, elk, and caribou numbers from overshooting the carrying capacity of the land. Equally important, wolves keep the ungulates moving. With the return of wolves, browsers become wary and mobile again, no longer lazily browsing lush areas (often decimating the wildflowers we humans like to see), but rather moving frequently — allowing plants to recover. This behavioral regulation of herbivores may be even more important than the numerical modification wolves provide. Wolves in the Northeast would probably mean slightly fewer deer in the Adirondacks and somewhat fewer moose in Maine but stronger individuals and healthier plant communities.

Although Adirondack forests have recovered beautifully from past destruction, and with them have returned beaver, fisher, moose, and other once-extirpated species, our top predators have not yet returned in functional numbers. Our trees have largely regrown, thanks to urgent conservation measures enacted in New York in the late 1800s after decades of massive logging, erosion, and burning; but we have not yet restored the forests' keystone carnivores. Still lacking their wild guardians, their original backcountry rangers, our forests are vulnerable to over-browsing by deer. Along with protecting wildlife habitat connections (wildways or wildlife corridors) within the Park and from the Park to wildlands beyond, we can help ensure that the Adirondacks stay forever wild by restoring missing species. As first steps, we should prevail upon the U.S. Fish & Wildlife Service and New York Department of Environmental Conservation to conduct feasibility studies, which should look at the ecological, economic, and social effects of carnivore recovery.

I believe the studies would show that such restoration would benefit native fauna and flora – especially songbirds, salamanders, wildflowers, and tree seedlings – and would make Adirondack Park a more pleasant and safer place for people to live. Without proposing a direct correlation between predator and prey numbers – Nature is more complex than that – I do suggest that restoring large carnivores and maintaining the big wild habitat cores and connections they need to thrive will benefit the ecology, economy, ethics, aesthetics, and health of Adirondack Park and Northern Appalachians.

European colonizers so fearfully and quickly eradicated wolves that we don't know for sure which species belongs here — red, gray, eastern, or some mix. We may be sure, though, the top dog would help keep our forests healthy. © Roderick MacIver Arts

Economic Benefits of Restoration

Wolves and cougars (and lynx and wolverine where climates remain cold and snowy enough) could enhance local and regional economies in at least two ways.

First, these top predators will allow hardwood forests to regenerate which will help wood products industries. In some parts of the East, over-browsing by deer has virtually halted hardwood regrowth. So far, the Adirondacks and Northern Appalachians have had cold and snowy enough winters to prevent massive deer overshoot, but with warming climate, we could face the same eating down of the forest that parts of the Southern and Central Appalachians are already facing. (For a preview of what our forests could look like with continued warming and too few top predators, walk Shawangunk or Hudson Valley woods in southeast New York, where you will find many thorny plants but few wildflowers or hardwood seedlings.)

Second, the return of our charismatic megafauna would attract numerous wildlife-watchers, bolstering the tourism industry. Hundreds of thousands of tourists a year visit Yellowstone National Park and Boundary Waters Canoe Area Wilderness in hopes of seeing, or at least hearing, a pack of wolves. Adirondack Park could become the Boundary Waters of the Northeast, if we welcome back the big animals we exterminated last century, to the enrichment of guides, hotel and restaurant owners, and other local businesspeople.

Social and Health Benefits of Ecological Restoration

Welcoming back the carnivores we shot out long ago would also benefit us ethically. Perhaps more than any other natural phenomena, carnivores test our decency, morality, and ethics. Generous people live and let live, all native species, even if some are at times vexing. Carnivores demand of us foresight and restraint, for they need big wild interconnected core habitats, protected from development, to flourish. I believe North Americans' response to large carnivores is one of the ultimate ethical tests of our time (along with addressing the larger but related extinction and climate crises).

The aesthetic benefits of restoring big wild cats and dogs are obvious to anyone who loves seeing beautiful animals in the wild. These gains, though, go way beyond the beauty of the creatures themselves (and it should be admitted: only a lucky few will ever so much as glimpse a cougar, so shy and elusive are they; even the more communal and louder wolves will be invisible to anyone not looking carefully). Return of top carnivores would mean healthier, richer wildflower and songbird populations. Our forests and streams will be more beautiful and more musical once carnivores have restored natural balances.

Finally, we come to some speculative but compelling reasons to restore carnivores: as agents of healthy balance, as hedges against outbreaks of zoonotic diseases. These hypotheses may not yet be provable, but the public health benefits of top carnivores patrolling our woods and waters might, once understood, persuade even the crustiest old gunners to let them live.

Carnivores will enhance public health in several ways: wolves and cougars will trim the deer population, which at present is unnaturally abundant in many parts of the East (due to elimination of large predators, fragmentation of forest, and supplemental feeding). In addition to inadvertently killing scores of Americans a year in collisions with cars, deer are also vectors for black-legged ticks, which carry Lyme disease and other afflictions.

As a personal aside: I've trekked thousands of miles across many of the wilder parts of North America, often in territory of grizzly and/or black bears, wolves, and big cats. The only carnivores who have ever given me any trouble are domestic dogs. The animals I fear most, by far, are ticks. I've had Lyme disease, and it scares me far more than do the toothiest beasts on the planet.

Some carnivores do occasionally prey on livestock, but this problem can be humanely addressed with careful husbandry, guard dogs and llamas, compensation programs for farmers who do lose animals, and realistic appraisal of relative risks. Feral dogs kill more livestock than do wolves or cougars. Still, consumers need to be willing to pay a little extra for predator-friendly meat and other ecologically responsible goods.

We'll ask in a later chapter the questions about which wolf the Northeast had (gray or red or both or something in between) and whether coyotes have begun to fill part of its niche. Is active reintroduction necessary, should we save the wildlife corridors that allow carnivores to recolonize on their own, or are both measures necessary? (I'd vote both.)

In short, for ecological and admittedly personal reasons, I believe that we ought to restore top carnivores in the East. Of course, we should not expect instant miracles. We've spent centuries exploiting and diminishing wild things; they and we will need a few decades to restore the balance. Cougars and wolves, and lynx and wolverine in boreal parts of our region, will help restore forest health, boost regional economies, enhance our ethical standing, beautify our environments, and keep us safer and healthier.

Chapter 2:
Beautiful Bobcats

Lynx rufus: Our Resilient Native Cat

Bobcats can easily be mistaken for large house-cats, being equally adorable in appearance. They are adaptable hunters of small animals, and can live near human settlements if allowed.
© *Larry Master, www.masterimages.org*

People have too oft neglected or persecuted cats. When early human colonizers arrived in North America millennia ago, this great land was graced with many cat species, including American lion, American cheetah (why pronghorn "antelope" in American West can run 60 miles per hour), saber-tooth cats (perhaps several species), jaguar, cougar, jaguarundi, ocelot, margay cat, lynx, and bobcat. Grab your favorite paleo-biology text, and look up these

28

long-time North American denizens. You will be inspired by their beauty and chagrined that our forebears killed off most of them (in numbers, if not species).

American lion and cheetah and sabre-tooth cats fell victim to human overkill, at least indirectly, as early human colonizers used new weapons to rapidly kill mega-herbivores, like woolly mammoth and mastodon, for food and fiber, leaving native predators much less food. Two big cats in North America, puma (cougar) and jaguar, survived in the West, and most of the small cats survived in diminished ranges and numbers.

Lynx rufus in Our Region

The North American wild cat who has proved most tolerant of human interlopers is *Lynx rufus*, bobcat, whose range still includes most of North America south of the boreal forest. Bobcats can thrive in habitats as varied as Georgia's Okefenokee Swamp (where I saw my first bobcat, decades ago), northern Minnesota's sub-boreal forests, and central California's chaparral and grasslands (where I used to see them commonly in Golden Gate National Recreation Area, where wildlife is fully protected thus not so fearful of people).

Bobcats in our area like rocky hills for dens and sunning places, woods and meadows for hunting rodents and rabbits, swamps for hunting muskrats, and frozen ponds, for patrolling edges where small rodents may appear. They can live fairly near people but generally avoid getting too close to us. Perhaps because they've evolved a fear of tool-wielding bipedal mammals, they are most active at night and dawn and dusk (though I've been lucky to see them in broad daylight several times on lands protected by Northeast Wilderness Trust, Eddy Foundation, Champlain Area Trails, and Adirondack Land Trust here in Split Rock Wildway).

Why Bobcats Should Be Protected

Imagine your housecat at her finest, add fifteen pounds of muscle and brain, make her even more symmetrical and athletic, shorten her tail, enhance her beauty, and you have the basic image of a bobcat. Do you wish to shoot her or entrap her in steel jaws? You do not, thank goodness, but your tax-payer-funded wildlife officials don't mind if you do.

Despite strong public sentiment in favor of protecting bobcats, the New York Department of Environmental Conservation a few years ago expanded the killing season on bobcats, apparently under pressure from a small number of sport-hunters and trappers who wanted to take more wildcat pelts. Most other states in the Northeast also have killing seasons on bobcats, notwithstanding the growing body of science showing the ecological importance of predators and how vulnerable they are to social or population disruption if heavily shot or trapped.

New Hampshire has lately been protecting its bobcats, and the Granite State is the richer for it. Recurring efforts by sports to open a killing season on bobcats there, as well as ongoing killing seasons on bobcats in New York and other states, are unfortunate, for ecological, aesthetic, ethical, and recreational reasons.

Many of the once widespread wild cats of North America have been persecuted so heavily that their ranges and numbers have dramatically decreased. The bobcat has been luckier than most, persevering or recovering in our region, partly because it is relatively tolerant of humans. The people pushing to begin or extend killing seasons on this predator overlook its important role in natural ecosystems, as well as its inherent beauty.

Bobcats play important ecological roles in forest ecosystems. They are effective predators of rodents and rabbits, helping hold in check numbers of these and other plant-eaters. Bobcats occasionally take deer, usually weak ones, at a time when over-browsing by deer (who have lost their main natural predators, cougars and wolves) threatens to degrade our eastern deciduous Forest.

In general, persecution of carnivores is wrong, again for ecological and ethical reasons. Carnivores generally reproduce slowly, have few natural predators, and are intelligent animals with complex social organizations. Most parts of our country suffer from too many herbivores and too few predators. We should be protecting, not persecuting, our remaining predators and studying how to restore those we've eradicated.

The once-eradicated predators of the Northeast include the bobcat's more boreal cousin, the Canada lynx (*Lynx canadensis*); and its imperiled status is another reason why allowing the killing of bobcats, by guns or traps, is wrong. Bobcats and lynx look much alike; and sport hunters or trappers can easily kill lynx thinking they are killing bobcat.

Lynx have survived in northern Maine and have been seen in recent years in northern New Hampshire and Vermont. Combined with climate warming, a killing season on bobcats could doom long-term viability of lynx (which primarily prey on snowshoe hares and need cold snowy winters to thrive) in our region and make extremely unlikely their recolonization of the Adirondacks.

A Lifetime Thrill: Backtracking a Beautiful Bobcat

Like house cats, bobcats enjoy basking in the sun, especially in winter, when finding sunny sheltered spots minimizes the energy they need to burn to keep warm. © Sheri Amsel, www.exploringnature.org

Moreover, bobcats are just plain beautiful! Like all conservationists, I hope people will value wildlife for its natural beauty and intrinsic value. Even if some must look at wildlife and wild places through a utilitarian lens, though, protecting bobcats makes sense. They are worth more for wildlife watching and tracking opportunities than they are as pelts or meat.

Rare and lucky is the person who catches more than a fleeting glimpse of this gorgeous cat. A lifetime's thrill can be more easily found, though, by humbly backtracking a bobcat on a frozen swamp, reading the hunter's story in prints, how she investigates muskrat lodges, down logs, snags, and anywhere else she may find a vole or mouse or rabbit to feed the kittens inside her.

Chapter 3:
Missing Cats of Our Home
What Prospects for Cougar and Lynx?

Cougars are among the Americas' greatest athletes, with leaping and sprinting abilities far greater than those of Olympians. © Larry Master, www.masterimages.org

We ought to share our Adirondack home with at least three species of wild cats: cougar, lynx, and bobcat. Unkindly, we have extirpated cougar and lynx, and allow bobcat to be trapped and hunted every winter. See the last chapter for more on bobcats.

Our larger North American home is also home for jaguar, ocelot, margay cat, and jaguarundi, in subtropical regions; however, humans have greatly diminished populations of all these wild cats, through direct persecution and habitat destruction. Early human settlers of North America probably played major roles in the demise of American lion, American cheetah, and saber-tooth tiger. We may not have dared to hunt these great predators with our spears, but we overhunted – unto extinction – the great herbivores (from giant beavers the size of small cars to woolly mammoths of elephant kin) that were the predators' food, with our simple yet deadly weapons.

Our relations with cats, then, are strained, despite the great love many of us feel for our companion cats and despite the great beauty most of us see in wild felines. Much of what I know about cats I've learned by watching our family cats and by tracking with Susan Morse, founder of one of our continent's premier citizen science groups, Keeping Track (keepingtrack.org). Sue is among North America's top wildlife trackers, and she has introduced thousands of students, of all ages, to the joys of following wildlife and to the knowledge tracking can add to the natural history that underlies biodiversity conservation.

Supporting Our Local Athletes

Sue taught me about the precision jumps bobcats and cougars make to reach safe ground, descend cliffy terrain, or pounce on prey. A ledge-jumper myself, I am in awe of the leaps wild cats make in the course of their everyday travels and hunting. (I've an uncharacteristically commercial idea for some cool company, like Patagonia or Black Diamond: a beautiful athlete, wearing snowshoes, is leaping off a high ledge into deep snow; the photographer catches her half-way down, snow flying everywhere; the caption reads: *Snow is fine. Air is essential.* All proceeds of gear sold through this ad go to protecting wild cat habitat!)

Like their larger distant cousins, cougars (*Puma concolor*), bobcats (*Felis rufus*) are native to most of the East, but unlike cougars and lynx (*Felis canadensis*, which are native to much of North America's boreal forest but have lost most of their habitat south of Canada), bobcats are faring relatively well in the East in areas not too badly fragmented. Here at home in Split Rock Wildway I'll get lucky and see one of these elusive cats a few times a decade. Much more often, fairly regularly in winter, I find bobcat tracks in snow on my frozen pond or nearby wetlands. Despite being much smaller than cougars (and comparable in size to lynx, though without such long legs and big feet as their boreal cousins), bobcats do occasionally take deer during winter in the north. Sue has documented bobcat kills of white-tailed deer, and she vividly describes how a cat can pounce from above on the neck of a deer slowed down by deep snow (probably a small, weak, sick, or aged deer, given the size imbalance), and sever the carotid artery to effect a quick kill.

With their greater size and power, cougars are much more effective predators of deer, and can accomplish the life-exchanging sacrifice with a crushing bite to the spinal cord. Very few people ever witness the athletic prowess of wild North American cats hunting (just once, I had the thrill of watching a mother bobcat lead her two kittens in stalking wood ducks in a swamp near my cabin), but to hear and see Sue describe the process with her words and photos is to almost be there. Sue feels that cougars have good habitat and ample prey in many of the wilder parts of the East, but they need safe travel corridors to return here.

As Will Stolzenburg describes in his book, *Heart of a Lion*, at least one heroic cougar has made the incredible journey eastward from the Midwest in recent years. A young male cougar in 2009 set out from the Black Hills of South Dakota, seeking a home territory with a mate as he wandered eastward. Wildlife camera photos and genetic evidence allowed biologists to roughly trace his route as he made his way to the Adirondacks in the winter of 2011. There, he likely found ample prey and good cover, but no mate, so he resumed traveling, only to be tragically hit and killed by a car in Connecticut later that year.

Many Adirondack residents are sure they've seen a cougar, and this wild wanderer from the Black Hills may be the one some folks have seen. As mentioned in chapter one, we probably do have cougars at least traveling through the Adirondacks occasionally (young males looking for mates, as with this Black Hills cat, or possibly an occasional released individual kept as a pet till he or she got too big), but we almost certainly do not have a breeding, functioning, preying population of cougars in the U.S. East north of Florida, where a small population of the great cats (there called panthers) persists.

What Prospects for Northern Feline Neighbors?

Lynx seem to be fairing a little better in the Northeast, with a sizable population in northern Maine and increased sightings of them in northern New Hampshire and Vermont. They probably belong here in the Adirondacks, too, but climate warming may make recovery of this boreal species problematic. The New York Department of Environmental Conservation tried unsuccessfully two decades ago to restore lynx to the Adirondacks, but most of the cats were quickly killed. They'd been live-trapped in the Yukon, where they had no familiarity with human dangers, like roads, cars, and farms; so quickly ran into troubles as they dispersed from their High Peaks release site. Biologists have learned much about successful wild carnivore releases since then, in part through a successful lynx recovery program in the Colorado Rockies, but our warming climate leaves in question whether another lynx recovery here is feasible over the long run – a question we should study.

Lynx seem to have co-evolved with their primary prey, snowshoe hare, with matching big paws and amazing agility to race and swerve across the snow. © Larry Master, www.masterimages.org

I personally would recommend that New Yorkers and New Englanders and their state wildlife departments end the killing seasons on bobcats, study where and how lynx recovery might be achievable, and begin working with local residents to prepare for a much needed reintroduction of cougars to wilder parts of our region. Wildlife corridors are necessary but not sufficient for the protection and recovery of the apex predators we've unkindly eliminated. Along with conserving big wild connected habitats for them, we also need to actively reach out and welcome home these missing cats.

For many years, conservationists have been urging federal and state wildlife officials to expand the recovery range for the Florida panther (same cat as cougar, puma, mountain lion, and catamount) and to study the reintroduction potential for cougar in other wild parts of the East. So far, we've been politely dismissed, partly due to misplaced fears on the part of some people and general lack of awareness of the importance of native carnivores. Contrary to misconceptions sometimes spread by sensationalized media accounts, welcoming cougars back into our wild forests of the Southeast Coastal Plain, Appalachians, and Adirondacks would make our lives *safer*, as well as our forests more beautiful.

Chapter 4:
Coyotes and Other Canids
Welcoming the Coywolf, Whoever It May Be

Unfairly persecuted across our country, coyotes (sometimes called song dogs) are among the most musical, intelligent, and resourceful of carnivores, and help keep populations of smaller mammals in check. © Sheri Amsel, www.exploringnature.org

By now, most of us who spend much time outside in Adirondack Park have seen some sort of large canid (dog family member) that looks too big to be a coyote, not quite big enough to be a wolf. Likely, many of us have seen what some wildlife observers are calling the *coywolf,* an evocative name for what some scientists prefer to call the *eastern coyote.*

39

The coywolf, or eastern coyote, is a skilled predator combining the wily nature of the coyote (*Canis latrans*) with a healthy mixture of eastern wolf (*Canis lupus lycaon*). The inter-breeding between coyotes and wolves in eastern North America has resulted in a canid with the resourcefulness of the smaller cousin but also with some of the heft and pack-hunting ability of wolves. Because of big dogs' penchant for roaming, our region's coywolves, or eastern coyotes, may also have some genes from our beloved domestic dogs, resulting in more nerve around humans. Research and debate continue, but recent genetic testing suggests that these hybrid canids are probably on average something like two-thirds coyote, nearly one-third wolf, and a small fraction domestic dog.

How the coywolf emerged is a long, fascinating, and somewhat mysterious story. To greatly oversimplify, eastern North America originally had two or three wolf species, at least one of which (now known as red wolf and surviving in tiny, imperiled numbers in coastal North Carolina) was closely related genetically to the coyote. When European settlers eradicated our large wolf species, they left a void that coyotes moved in from the west to fill.

As coyotes colonized eastern North America, they occasionally interbred with remnant wolf populations in eastern Canada, and then moved south into the northeastern U.S. Coyotes in the U.S. Southeast apparently came by a more southerly route and did not interbreed with gray wolves (but do so now with red wolves), so are generally not as big as our northern coyotes. This muddles a bit the term 'eastern coyote,' which fails to recognize the difference from Northeast to Southeast.

Opportunity to Embrace Evolution

In my opinion, informed by thousands of miles of rambling eastern forests and listening to and reading the words of naturalists and biologists, it is time to celebrate this resourceful canid. Specifically we should:

* welcome the eastern coyote and/or coywolf,

* consider it a native top predator,

* and protect it as an integral part of healthy ecosystems.

Endlessly adaptable, coyotes apparently intermixed with reduced numbers of wolves as they spread eastward. The resulting eastern coyotes, or coywolves, have colonized most of the Northeast and could fill some of the niche left open after wolves were eradicated. © Larry Master, www.masterimages.org

The coywolf may be partly a consequence of human modifications of natural systems, but its emergence offers glorious evidence that evolution still works, even in our fragmented world.

However variable their genetic composition, coywolves are important regulators of prey populations that otherwise might grow out of balance, with harmful results for natural and human communities. Plus, these big wild dogs are beautiful creatures, worthy of our respect and admiration.

Wrong to Kill Coyotes, Wolves, and Coywolves

Against all ecological and ethical wisdom, most states in our country currently have open killing seasons on coyotes. The coyotes and coywolves we see in the Adirondacks and Vermont are heavily persecuted. While it may not significantly depress their numbers due to compensatory reproduction, persecution upsets their social dynamics and causes untold individual suffering.

Killing top predators is wrong for several reasons.

1. It doesn't work. If people are concerned about coyotes or coywolves killing livestock or house pets, it is wiser to allow wild canids to attain stable, self-regulating populations. Conflicts with domestic animals are most common in predator populations that are persecuted, such that the young do not have mature role models to teach them to hunt and keep clear of people.

2. Apex predators, particularly top carnivores, are essential members of healthy ecosystems. They help maintain herbivore populations and prevent them from over-browsing plant communities. In many parts of the East, our deciduous forests are now being browsed to the ground – to the detriment of songbird and wildflower populations as well as the trees themselves – by unnaturally high populations of white-tail deer. Such over-browsing is perhaps not yet so dire a problem here in Adirondack Park where we still sometimes have cold snowy winters, which limit deer numbers, but could become so as our

winters warm. We all love deer, and they too are important parts of forest ecosystems, but they have grown too abundant and lazy in the absence of their natural predators.

Coyotes do not fill the entire niche left by our past eradication of cougars and wolves, but they are beginning to fill some of that void. As noted repeatedly in this book, cougar and wolf recovery should also be considered top priorities for our region. Of note: a healthy wolf population would naturally hold in check coyote numbers.

Hunting by humans does not mimic hunting by native carnivores. Human hunters usually target the big strong "trophy" animals, whereas natural predators select the weak. The mere presence of top predators in an ecosystem keeps herbivores more alert and healthy and less prone to congregating in and over-browsing sensitive habitats.

3. So long as there's open killing season on coyotes, the real top dog, the wolf, has very little chance of successfully recolonizing our region from their remnant populations northward in Ontario and Quebec. All too often in areas wolves are trying to recolonize, they get shot by hunters claiming they thought they were shooting a coyote.

This type of mistaken identity has happened several times in the last few years in the West, most infamously in late 2014 when a gunner shot a female wolf in southern Utah, then got off without penalty (despite the gray wolf being listed under the Endangered Species Act) when he told wildlife officials he had thought he was shooting a coyote. The wolf had traveled all the way from Yellowstone to the Grand Canyon and had been named Echo by some of the school kids who were rooting for her. (I was lucky enough to see her, fleetingly, after fortuitously following part of her dispersal route southward.) Probably still looking for a mate, Echo drifted back north a little way into Utah, where she was shot.

Right now, if a wolf were to brave the major roads crossing southern Ontario just north of the St. Lawrence River (and perhaps cross the frozen river in a cold winter) and make it southeast into our beloved Adirondack Park, all too likely she would soon be shot for resembling a coyote.

Coyote packs in winter occasionally chase deer, especially ones weakened by hunger, onto ice where they are vulnerable to slipping. The carrion then feeds eagles and ravens, as well as the coyotes. © Larry Barns

4. Contrary to popular assumptions (based on outmoded but deep-seeded fears), native carnivores actually make our lives safer. Attacks by native carnivores on people are so rare as to be statistically irrelevant. Deer — excessively numerous because of insufficient natural predation — kill nearly two hundred Americans a year (mostly from vehicle-deer collisions). Domestic dogs kill about twenty Americans a year. But all native carnivores in the U.S. combined, might kill three in a bad year.

On the other hand, full complements of native carnivores help hold in check the vectors of zoonotic diseases. The prime example of this now is small rodents and deer spreading Lyme disease in fragmented ecosystems deficient in native carnivores. Lyme disease is a real threat to human health, exacerbated by our intolerance of wild predators.

5. Perhaps most important, native carnivores bring beauty and wholeness to our wild neighborhoods in ways aesthetic, ecological, recreational, ethical, and even spiritual. We will be a richer and happier people when we learn to coexist with all our native neighbors, coyotes, wolves, coywolves, and cougars included.

To get a taste of the joys of having these big toothy animals around, go out and follow their tracks in the snow some sunny winter day. It is highly unlikely that you will see tracks of cougar or full-bred wolf (if you do, please contact me!). But if you walk the protected lands and frozen waters of Split Rock Wildway you will see plenty of tracks from coyotes and/or coywolves, and likely also red or gray fox, bobcat, fisher, mink, or river otter.

If you are fortunate enough to track a coursing coyote, he or she (or both, for they often travel as couples in winter) will teach

45

you much about what these clever canids hunt (often rodents and rabbits, occasionally weak or old deer), what attracts their attention, where they scent-mark their territory, and much more. You will begin to learn the ways of one of our cleverest and handsomest neighbors.

Chapter 5:
Weasels of Our Home Lands and Waters
Strength Beyond Size

Weasels are quick and masterful hunters of rodents and other small animals, with high metabolisms that impel them to eat many. © Sheri Amsel, www.exploringnature.org

We are graced in Adirondack Park with at least six members of the weasel family, Mustelidae. The family of mustelids, in taxonomic terms, fits within the order Carnivora, which is in the class Mammalia, which is in the phylum Chordata, which is in the kingdom Animalia. We humans, of course, branched away from distant mammal relatives at the Order level, where we classify ourselves as Primates, and let the toothier ones be Carnivores.

As midsize or small carnivores, weasels subsist mainly on the meat of smaller animals. However, with their great quickness and agility, weasels can sometimes take prey bigger than themselves, as when an ermine takes a snowshoe hare or a wolverine takes an old deer. All these weasel family members are beautiful to behold, but most are elusive. You are fortunate if you glimpse one.

Weasels of our region, roughly in ascending order of size, include ermine (short-tailed weasel), long-tailed weasel, mink, marten, fisher, and river otter. Least weasels inhabit much of the northern United States and Canada, but apparently not the Adirondacks. Wolverines, the largest of North American weasels and a species that needs big wild places with cold snowy winters, likely inhabited snowy parts of our region but were extirpated from the East, south of Canada, decades ago.

Other members of the weasel family have rebounded somewhat in recent decades, with regrowth of once-cleared forest and with better wildlife management and water quality laws. We should not take their well-being for granted, however, as weasels are vulnerable to trapping and to habitat loss. Some may be particularly susceptible to human-caused climate chaos, too.

Aquatic Mustelids

Famously playful and smart, river otters are nonetheless vulnerable to traps, often set for beavers, and to water pollution. Healthy otter populations mean healthy waters. © Larry Master, www.masterimages.org

Our most charming weasel, those lucky enough to have seen one would probably agree, is the river otter (*Lontra canadensis*). These aquatic mustelids are amazingly deft and agile, swift enough under water to catch fish and frogs. Otters are most at home in water but will traverse land to reach other water bodies.

Sadly, otters sometimes are killed by cars as they try to cross roads – perhaps to reach a different waterway because the culvert through which the stream flows under the road is too small and clogged or has a dangerous spillover. Otters are also vulnerable to traps, often set for beavers but lethal to any aquatic mammal unlucky enough to enter the jaws. They are also harmed by water pollution.

In years past, I often saw otter tracks and slides in Split Rock Wildway during the winter. The last few winters, I've seen fewer otter tracks than previously. This may be mere chance, anecdotal observation that reflects no pattern, but I am worried. I miss seeing

49

the joyful otter slides on stream-banks and the playfully efficient bound-slide pulses across frozen wetlands. I fear a reversion to high rates of trapping for beaver pelts around here could ruin some of our richest ponds and wetlands and diminish otter and other aquatic wildlife numbers.

Mink you may have seen along the shores of Lake Champlain and its tributaries. Mink seem a bit more tolerant of people than some other weasels, though that tolerance can get them in trouble.

Years ago as I cycled home from work, I saw a confused mink on the road in front of the Ford car dealership in Elizabethtown. She was not there to get her car serviced, I'm sure, but likely had been moving up or down The Branch (which flows into the Boquet River just downstream) and had climbed up the stream bank at just the wrong time. I tried to shoo her back to the stream, but lost her behind a car and never knew whether she made it safely back to the water.

Mink tracks tend to be tidy angled twos, bounding in mud along streams or in snow across frozen wetlands or ponds. The tracks in winter often disappear into snow, doubtless in quest of tasty little rodents. I see mink tracks often in the Adirondacks along snowy or frozen waterways in winter; on the lucky occasions when I see a mink in the flesh, he or she is likely swimming or rock-hopping along the Split Rock Wild Forest shoreline.

Terrestrial Mustelids

Quick, brave, and agile, fishers commonly kill and eat porcupines, sometimes by chasing them up trees and lunging at the quilled rodent's face until he or she tires and falls. © Larry Master, www.masterimages.org

The fisher (*Martes pennanti,* though taxonomists may be changing this large weasel's scientific name) is our second biggest surviving mustelid, achieving sizes similar to those of a big house cat. (Perhaps this helps explain its popular nickname, "fisher-cat," despite *M. pennanti* being neither a fish-catcher nor a cat).

Every Adirondack camp owner should be delighted to see the rambling tracks of fisher (often in irregular clumps of three good-sized five-toed overlapping prints), for fishers are effective predators of porcupines and squirrels, which sometimes like to chew on or inhabit our log cabins.

Fishers do best in unbroken mature forests with plenty of snags and down logs, for homes and cover. In our region, fishers have made a comeback because once cleared lands have returned to forest. The Pacific fisher in the heavily logged Pacific Northwest has not been so fortunate, and it is an imperiled subspecies or population.

American marten (*Martes americana*), a smaller more boreal cousin to the fisher, live in the Adirondack High Peaks but probably seldom if ever come down to our oak-hickory or valley clay-plain forests. I was thrilled and surprised, though, to watch a marten scamper up a hemlock tree and watch me curiously from a high branch on Eddy Foundation land next to Hammond Pond Wild Forest during the summer of 2016 – and this area is only about a thousand feet in elevation! Still, marten are among the animals we need worry about as climate warms. Like their much larger distant cousins wolverines (*Gulo gulo*), marten do best in places with cold snowy winters. Also like most of their mustelid cousins, they are vulnerable to trapping.

If global demand for fur coats increases, trapping, combined with climate warming, could doom our High Peaks and western Adirondacks population of marten, though they are thought to be faring well at present. Indeed, the martens that I have encountered in the High Peaks, and that one I saw last year at lower elevation, have seemed more curious than frightened by my noisy passage.

The smaller weasels also tend to leave bounding tracks of angled twos, also in pursuit of small rodents. Ermine and long-tailed weasels are so quick, if you are lucky enough to glimpse one, she will probably disappear before you can so much as say hello. The last one I saw was a long-tailed weasel looking very vulnerable (to owls and larger predators) in her white winter coat in a snow-less December. She had ample habitat and prey around Coon Mountain, but I suspect the resident barred owl caught her before snow finally fell and made her camouflage work.

This poignant sighting reminded me of my friend Jerry Jenkins, brilliant naturalist and teacher, asking those of us taking one of his courses on plant communities of the West Champlain Hills: *What happens to a white rabbit* (snowshoe hare in winter pelage) *in a snowless winter, such as we'll see more and more of in this climate-change century?*

What happens to natural checks and balances when climate disruptions upset the evolutionary dance? If we let them, weasels may have special lessons to teach us, as we are forced to adjust to an overheating world of our own excess.

Chapter 6:
Beavers

Nature's Architects, a Keystone Species

Beavers live in extended family groups that may include several generations, gradually expanding their lodge system and watery domain, until the supply of young hardwoods runs low and they move on. © Sheri Amsel, www.exploringnature.org

Our region's largest rodent is also one of its most important ecological players. Beavers are what ecologists call a "keystone species," meaning they have disproportionate importance to their natural communities. They diversify ecosystems far more than their modest numbers would suggest.

The recovery of the North American beaver (*Castor canadensis*) across much of the northeastern United States, after being trapped out a century-plus ago, is among the great conservation success stories of American history. It is one we must not take for granted, though, as beavers are all too easy to trap and hunt out of a region.

Beavers are consummate ecosystem enhancers, rivaled in the West by prairie dogs. Through their dam-building and tree-trimming work, beavers create ponds and wetlands, which in turn serve a wide range of wildlife, from dragonflies to trout to otters to songbirds. In our part of the world, where wildfire is not a common natural disturbance agent, beavers are (along with wind-throw and ice storms) critical creators of natural openings that (unlike clear-cuts) provide natural edge habitat without bringing in exotic species and pollution.

We are fortunate in the Adirondacks to have goodly numbers of beavers, fostering pond and wet-meadow ecosystems that are among the richest in the Northeast. I am especially lucky that my Adirondack home is next to a beaver pond, and the many hours I have spent watching these robust rodents have left me in awe. Defying textbook prescriptions, they have merrily dined on hemlock saplings, even while young hardwoods stood nearby; and they have, to my untrained eyes at least, directionally-felled large trees to within inches of my cabin and woodshed. This I take to be an apt warning: I am welcome on their land so long as I respect their authority.

Next time you hear a landowner or road-worker complain of the nuisances caused by beavers, please urge them to reach for their binoculars rather than their guns or traps. Where beaver floods cannot be brooked, beaver-deceivers and other exclusionary devices provide benign alternatives to killing our keystone neighbors.

Remember, too, restoring apex predators to our region, cougar and wolf especially, will help assure that beaver numbers remain complementary to our native trees and flowers.

Chapter 7:
Porcupines
Prickly Tree Sculptors

Porcupines prune hemlocks and also eat the bark of some hardwood trees, making them an important natural disturbance agent in northern forests. © Sheri Amsel, www.exploringnature.org

I see more porcupines in the average month around my home in the Adirondacks than I saw in a year and a half trekking the Eastern and Western Wildways, though on those long conservation journeys I hiked through thousands of miles of forest that looked plenty inviting for bark-eaters. Teacher and fellow rambler Jerry Jenkins, author of the *Northern Forest Atlas Project*, has half seriously proposed that here in the Adirondacks at least, porcupines – not quite the largest, but surely the pointiest of North American rodents – may be a keystone species.

As mentioned last chapter, *keystone species* are those that play disproportionately great roles in their ecosystems and enhance overall diversity. Examples, again, are beavers here in forested areas and prairie dogs in western grasslands, both of which enrich natural habitats through their building and feeding habits; and wolves and cougars, which regulate herbivore behavior and abundance.

North American porcupines (*Erethizon dorsatum*; relatives of several similar quilled species of South America and Africa) may indeed play major herbivory roles here in the Adirondacks, where our forests grow much hemlock and hardwood. Porcupines feed heavily on hemlock branches and deciduous tree bark. Almost like climbing beavers, porcupines sometimes eat so much of a hardwood tree's bark that they effectively girdle and eventually kill the tree. An individual porcupine may have a favorite hemlock that she climbs most days for weeks, eventually pruning it into a new, more compact shape. Dead trees, of course, provide food and become homes for woodpeckers and cavity nesters, from chickadees to fishers, the main predator of porcupines.

High Numbers of Porcupines in Adirondacks

Why do we seem to have so many porcupines in the Adirondacks? I suspect this quilled rodent may be more abundant now than it was in earlier centuries because, unfortunately, our forebears exterminated cougars and greatly reduced fishers and bobcats, the animals that eat porcupines.

These days, the main killer of porcupines is the automobile, with many dark slow rodents meeting a tragic demise while crossing a road, or licking salt from the side of the road, at night.

I enjoy seeing porcupines, and I always chuckle as they give an almost embarrassed look when unsuspectingly being spotted half-way up a tree. I also smile when I see partially debarked trees, often American beeches, high on a slope or ridge. The gnawing can look much like that typically done by beavers, and sometimes for a moment I think: how came a beaver way up here so far from water? Then I realize (from the shallower chewing and the higher location) that the sculptor was the beaver's distant relative the porcupine, adding lighter colors to the grays and browns of tree trunks and branches.

Sometimes, porcupines, unlike other browsers, climb all the way to the tops of tall trees to eat the more succulent tree branches or bark, sculpting more diversity into the forest.

Welcoming Prickly Neighbors

Some of my neighbors do not look upon porcupines so favorably, however, because of their penchant for chewing wood — occasionally including wood that people have fashioned for their own purposes. Having your porch supports gnawed by a porcupine is annoying, but there are benign ways (like wire mesh, hot pepper, or ammonia) to discourage rodents from chewing wood.

I hope we will welcome porcupines as being important members of our region's forest communities. I urge we also protect their midsize natural predators, fisher and bobcat, and welcome home their largest native predator, the cougar. Collectively, these predators can keep porcupine numbers in check, while allowing them to continue their arboreal sculpting.

Chapter 8:
Moose

Recovery in Doubt

Moose can disperse long distances, and one cow moose — named Alice by her followers — was documented moving from the central Adirondacks to Ontario's Algonquin Park, confirming the Adirondack to Algonquin (A2A) wildlife corridor that conservationists advocated protecting. Maybe the Algonquin bull moose depicted here met Alice! © Roderick MacIver Arts

The biggest animal to recolonize our region after past extirpation is the moose. The largest member of the deer family (Cervidae), moose (*Alces alces*) hint at the Pleistocene mega-fauna that for epochs prior to arrival of *Homo sapiens* (humans) shaped North American ecosystems. Sadly, our early hunting forebears wiped out most of the great mammals, including mammoths, glyptodonts, ground sloths, and five-hundred-pound beavers. Moose survived the Pleistocene overkill, but they were for a time relegated to more northerly areas.

Moose have since made an amazing comeback in our region, but their future is far from certain. Moose are a boreal animal and suffer greatly in hot weather. A warming world will not be kind to moose.

Already, in southern parts of their reclaimed original range, particularly in New England and Minnesota, moose are suffering from devastating infestations of moose ticks. Like many furred animals, moose commonly carry ticks, and moose ticks are apparently a native species that specializes in parasitizing the huge deer. Moose ticks are becoming unnaturally abundant, with generally milder winters allowing their populations to surge.

In a heart-rending, paradoxical tragedy, some moose these days are freezing to death, after rubbing off their fur in response to huge tick loads. On some down or weakened moose, researchers have counted tens of thousands of the blood-sucking arthropods. The great tracker Sue Morse, founder of Keeping Track, showed photos at a wildlife show at the Whallonsburg Grange a couple years ago of bloody snow-beds where moose had lain down, squishing enough of the blood-gorged ticks on their belly to leave dark red stains in the snow. This is climatic injustice, a sad reminder of the misery we are already causing other creatures through upsetting natural climate as well as diminishing natural habitat.

Absence of Predators Leads to Suffering

The climate part of this sad story has been told many places. Not so often acknowledged is the predator part of the story – or absence from the story. When they lose their native predators, herbivores eventually suffer, as they over-browse their plant communities. Wolves have been eradicated from most of the East, including the parts of the Northeast that moose have recolonized in recent decades. Wolves are the main natural predator of moose. In the absence of wolves, moose have reached unnaturally high numbers in northern Maine and likely elsewhere. They are overeating the trees and shrubs. This leaves them malnourished and more susceptible to heavy parasite loads.

In short, to assure moose a healthy long future in our region, we need to curtail carbon emissions to minimize global warming and reintroduce missing top predators. For controlling white-tail deer numbers, cougars are probably most important. For controlling moose numbers, wolves are most important.

Today's Adirondack Moose

Moose's long legs and large hooves serve them well in the wetlands they browse in summer and the snowy forest they browse in winter. © Sheri Amsel, www.exploringnature.org

Moose have slowly recolonized our beloved Adirondack Park over the last couple decades, coming from Vermont and Quebec. Moose numbers in northern New York are thought to exceed 500 now. We have large amounts of prime moose habitat in northern

New York, including expansive wetlands and northern hardwood and spruce/fir forest.

Moose like to browse wetland plants, especially in the heat of summer, when cool water is more comfortable than hot muggy air. You may find their tracks and tooth marks from browsing in upland hardwoods at any time of year, and you may also be surprised to find their huge prints and long gate in deep snow in spruce/fir forest fairly high in the mountains. Cold does not bother these boreal giants, and moderately deep snow is no problem with their long legs. Conifers in winter are some of the tastiest things around for the largest terrestrial vegetarians our region still supports.

I have been lucky enough to see moose only a few times in the Adirondacks (many more times in Maine and Alaska): first a mother and sub-adult offspring in Cedar River Flow; most recently a big cow moose near Lake Placid. But my most surprising moose sighting was here in Split Rock Wildway, where many years ago arch-rambler Gary Randorf led me on a "random scoot" which took us to some huge hoof-prints that resolved themselves into a massive dark deer in dense foliage who fled from us as we approached her, near Salamander Swamp.

On a wildlife camera on Eddy Foundation land near Parch Pond, we got two nice photos of a young bull moose walking toward Hammond Pond Wild Forest last year. Also, Jamie Phillips and I found fresh moose tracks a few years ago on the land Champlain Area Trails soon after purchased and protected as the Wildway Passage parcel.

So far, fortunately, moose in New York's Adirondack Park seem to be faring relatively well against the rising moose tick problem, perhaps because their numbers are still well below carrying capacity. Moose ticks here are apparently not such a problem as they are in Maine.

Moose in New York are protected, because their numbers here are still low. Maine, New Hampshire, and Vermont have hunting seasons on moose, and rifle-hunters pay significant amounts of money into state wildlife management budgets for permits to shoot the biggest possible quarry. In Alaska and some parts of Canada, families depend on "bagging" a moose or two for their winter's meat.

As noted elsewhere, though, hunting by humans seldom if ever mimics hunting by wild predators. We humans tend to gun for the biggest "trophy" animals, whereas wild predators usually target the weak or sick, thus strengthening the herd.

Section 2:

Slithering, Crawling, and Hopping Things

Split Rock Wildway is not just land; it is also water. Ideally, habitat connections will continue along and across Lake Champlain. Animals crossing the lake to or from Split Rock Wildway may find forested habitat along the tributary streams, including on the Vermont side: Lewis, Otter, and Little Otter Creeks. © Bill Amadon

For many people, "wildlife" means large mammals. Big ungulates and carnivores may indeed be the most charismatic wildlife, from our human perspective, but *wild life* includes animals and plants and other life-forms of diverse sorts. All of these species deserve equal rights to their native homes.

Protecting the turtles, snakes, frogs, salamanders, insects, and other oft-overlooked wildlife means protecting their natural homes, their habitat, which usually in our region means forest-land and associated waters. It also means minimizing pollution and road-kill. (I focus more on road ecology in the final section of this book.)

Here we simply offer quick looks at a few of the reptiles and amphibians you may encounter on walks or paddles in Split Rock Wildway or the larger Adirondack Park. Any of us could spend our whole life learning our amphibious and scaled neighbors, and we would be the richer for it. Even knowing just a few of the more common "creepy-crawlies" helps us to understand our home better. So head into the woods with a field guide, and poke around a bit. Find some salamanders and frogs and turtles, and try to appreciate the challenges they and their families face in the fragmented world we have wrought.

Chapter 9:
Serpentine Splendors
Snakes of the Adirondack Champlain Valley

Garter snakes are the serpents we see most often in Split Rock Wildway, though we have several other equally splendid species. All of them help regulate numbers of small rodents.
© *Larry Master, www.masterimages.org*

Here on the equable Adirondack Coast, we are blessed with more snake species than in colder parts of the Northeast. By northern forest standards we are fairly rich in amphibians, especially salamanders, but like most cool areas, we have only modest numbers of reptile species. The excellent field guide *Amphibians and Reptiles of New York State* puts Champlain Valley tallies at about ten frogs and toads, eleven salamanders, five turtles, nine snakes, and a skink.

Daintiest of our snakes is the smooth green snake. I have seen only two in my years of rambling the Adirondacks: one on

Treadway Mountain in Pharoah Lake Wilderness and one atop Rattlesnake Mountain north of Willsboro. We are more likely to see common garter snakes, often in woods near our homes; eastern ribbon snakes, frequenting marshes and pond edges; and northern water snakes, which we may glimpse swimming near shore in Lake Champlain. Here, too, but elusive, are redbelly snake, ring-necked snake, milk snake, and brown snake.

Crotalus horridus

Handsomest of our native snakes is the timber rattlesnake, which is often the color of a quiet summer evening here in the hills along Lake Champlain, a charcoal gray that could make you think it a different species from the yellowish varieties farther south. This dark color helps the ectothermic ("cold-blooded") serpent absorb the sun's warmth.

I have seen perhaps twenty rattlesnakes in all my years of rambling Split Rock Wildway. Notwithstanding their frightful scientific name, usually they've been lying shyly coiled in a patch of sun in the woods, basking and watching for rodents to eat. Several times, I've come upon rattlesnakes while cycling Lakeshore Road. Each time I have gingerly urged the snake safely away from the road. Thrice I was too late, as people driving heedlessly fast already had run over the snakes.

This would need study to prove, but I suspect Lakeshore Road is to some degree a barrier to dispersal of rattlesnakes, which den together in winter near the lake but move inland in summer, sometimes as far as Webb Royce Swamp. Historically, timber rattlesnakes surely had a range extending at least as far north as the eponymous mountain north of Willsboro and likely at least as far west as Coon Mountain, the rocky south slopes of which offer ideal snake habitat.

Somehow surviving decades of pointless persecution, rattlesnakes in their northern reaches appear to be limited in distribution to Split Rock Wild Forest and nearby private lands. A little way south, timber rattlesnakes also keep rodents honest in Lake George Wild Forest. Thankfully the New York Department of Conservation protects timber rattlesnakes as a threatened species. So it is illegal, as well as unethical, to kill them.

If you come upon a rattlesnake on your land and do not want it there, please call the DEC. They will translocate it back to the nearby Wild Forest.

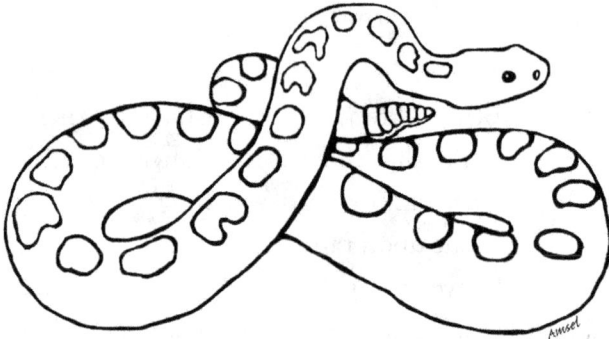

We are fortunate in Split Rock Wildway to have one of the northern-most populations of timber rattlesnake. They like the rocky slopes and sunny glades of Split Rock Wild Forest.
© *Sheri Amsel, www.exploringnature.org*

Risks: Rattlesnakes vs. Ticks

Never have I felt at all threatened by rattlesnakes, not even the greater numbers I have seen out West, some of which are not as docile as our timber rattlesnakes. (Even the one I nearly stepped on while descending Arizona's Mt. Graham at dusk years ago merely rattled, with no intent to strike.) We are much too big to be prey for any North American snake, and they do not want to waste precious venom striking us. They just want us to let them be.

We are at much greater risk from the ticks carried by many rodents (primary snake food) than we are from snakes or larger predators, which generally safeguard our forests by controlling the populations of animals that serve as vectors for Lyme disease and other afflictions. Indeed, I would hazard a guess that snakes enhance public health by keeping rodent numbers in check.

Chapter 10:
Turtles

Old Neighbors in Mobile Homes

Most colorful of our common turtles is the painted turtle, which often basks on sunny logs in ponds and wetlands of our region. © Larry Master, www.masterimages.org

We are fortunate to have in the Champlain Basin at least six turtle species. You may not see the rarer ones: spotted turtle, common musk turtle (or "stinkpot"), northern map turtle, and eastern spiny softshell. Several additional turtle species are native to New York State, but their populations mostly are found further to the south or west of our region.

I have been lucky enough to see several map turtles at the mouth of the Boquet River and once to glimpse a spiny softshell. I occasionally see our more numerous shelled neighbors, the painted turtle and common snapping turtle (*Chelydra serpentine*) while rowing or rambling around Lake Champlain.

72

All but the painted and snapping turtles are sadly diminished in numbers in our area due to habitat destruction and fragmentation, pollution, and road-kill. Although those two species still seem fairly abundant, we should take care to conserve their habitats and avoid hitting them when they try to cross roads, lumbering slowly as they carry their shelters with them. As fellow residents of the eastern United States, we should take pride in our turtle diversity. A large fraction of the world's 240 or so turtle species (belonging to the ancient order Testudinata) live in our part of the world.

Let us look a little more closely at our one local turtle who may scare you, the snapping turtle, in the hopes that you will learn to appreciate them more. Our snapping turtle is small compared to the alligator snapping turtle of the Southeast Coastal Plain and Mississippi River drainage, which may top 150 pounds in weight and has a massive head with fiercely hooked beak!

Our Scary Turtle

Common snapping turtles look mean but are not a threat to people or our companion animals unless we behave recklessly around them. Our snapping turtles may reach 14 inches in carapace length and 45 pounds in weight, occasionally larger. Generally speaking, the bigger the turtle, the older it is. Most turtles are long-lived, as well as belonging to an order that long predates our own. If left in peace, turtles may live many decades.

Snapping turtles do indeed snap and lurk below the surface in murky waters, giving fright to small waterfowl and timid skinny-dippers. In truth, snapping turtles subsist largely on plants, and their most common animal prey is likely to be crayfish. It would be maladaptive for them to attack any animal too big to easily fit in their beak-like mouths.

But if you corner a snapper on land, she may indeed lunge at you in self defense. I generally carry thick work gloves when I cycle or drive on rural roads, in case I come across a turtle trying to cross the road. I gingerly carry them safely off the road, holding them by the sides of the carapace with the head well away from me. They protest harmlessly and are saved from being killed by cars.

Snapping turtles are the heftiest of our native reptiles, but despite their fierce appearance, they are shy and subsist largely on vegetation. © Larry Master, www.masterimages.org.

Such a traveling turtle is likely to be a female looking for a place to lay her eggs. Untold countless thousands of turtles are killed on roads in our country every year, in part because many of them, including snapping turtles, like to lay their eggs in sandy soils well above the water.

Disease, Habitat Destruction & Climate Change

Turtles are vulnerable not only to killing by cars and habitat destruction but also to diseases from released pet turtles and from climate chaos. Unnaturally high temperatures can disrupt the gender ratio of turtle populations. As noted in *The Amphibians and Reptiles of New York State,* an excellent field guide published by Oxford University Press, "Nest temperatures higher than 84 degrees F produce primarily females, whereas lower temperatures produce predominantly males."

The susceptibility of turtles to introduced diseases and to warming temperatures are reminders of the sensitivity of the natural world to human machinations, and they are added reasons for us to conserve as much wild habitat as possible and pollute as little as possible.

Chapter 11:
Frogs
Amphibious Songsters

Green frogs' banjo-like plunks are a regular part of our midsummer music in Adirondack Park, helping fill the transition from spring bird-song to late summer insect-song. © Larry Master, www.masterimages.org

By late April, spring peepers have begun warming up for their mating choruses along the beaver pond near my home in Split Rock Wildway. Wood frogs begin singing, if duck-like quacks be song, from vernal pools in the eastern Adirondacks even before the winter ice is all melted. Gray treefrogs, color-shifting cousins of the peepers, start their mating trills in May and continue them intermittently through summer.

Here in Adirondack Park we are fortunate to live among frogs, yet for all the thousands we hear each evening, we may go weeks without seeing any. Spring peepers' chorus gets so loud that by early May when my family sits on our porch near the pond, we cannot talk over the glorious din. Yet if I try to find even just one of these tiny songsters, I usually fail, seeming to create a brief wave of silence as I walk along the pond.

Gray treefrogs do not sound so vast a chorus, but they also are much more often heard than seen with their mating calls often emanating from somewhere up in the trees. You can look right at one and not see it, for they change their skin color to match the background of green leaf, brown ground, or gray bark.

In late spring, amphibian choirs will be enhanced by American toads, with their many-voice rising trills; and northern leopard frogs, with growl-like mating calls which fit their common name; and pickerel frogs, similar to leopard frogs in appearance and voice, but with their splotches along their backs more square in pattern. Green frogs will pluck like banjos and bull frogs will bellow like their namesakes on summer evenings – the males calling for females even after a first generation of pollywogs nears maturation. In colder parts of Adirondack Park, mink frogs are part of the anuran music.

Frogs, by the way, are good neighbors not only for their lovely music but for their habit of eating mosquitoes and leeches and other creatures we find disagreeable. Susceptible to habitat degradation, frogs also betray our environmental transgressions.

Living in the Adirondack woods, frog-song is nearly as much a part of our sonic environment as is birdsong. It is likewise a fragile source of music.

Even as we have diminished songbird populations by fragmenting their forest habitats (on summer breeding grounds where we live and on winter grounds in Central and South

American rainforests), we have reduced and polluted frog habitat by building roads and dams and putting toxic chemicals, sediments, and exotic species into waterways. We also too often kill individual frogs when we drive rural roads on warm rainy spring nights, when frogs and salamanders migrate to breeding pools.

Frog-song makes spring special, and frogs are key players in healthy forest and pond ecosystems. Let us save wild forests and free-flowing waterways to keep our hopping neighbors healthy.

Chapter 12:
Searching for Skinks
Lizards of the Forest

Five-lined skinks, rare as far north as we are, often live in the rocky woodlands that timber rattlesnakes also favor. © Sheri Amsel, www.exploringnature.org

Most of us think of lizards as reptiles of sparse deserts, and indeed, North American deserts have most of our continent's lizard species. Temperate North America does, however, have a family of lizards, called skinks, which mostly inhabit forests and grasslands. Just one of these species, so far, inhabits Adirondack Park, most of the others being more southerly.

If Split Rock Wildway does not have skinks, it may soon, in a warming world. I have seen ground skinks (*Scincella lateralis*) on my rambles in the Southeast, and I have heard rumors of five-lined skinks (*Eumeces fasciatus*) here on the Adirondack Coast, but I have never seen a skink north of Kentucky. Have you? A fellow Champlain Area Trails walker reported seeing skinks in forest outside of Ticonderoga, not far south of Split Rock Wildway.

Are the rumors true that five-lined skinks form symbiotic relationships with timber rattlesnakes? If so, that alliance, together with range maps going north up the Hudson Valley and a warming climate, would suggest our future may be enriched by this smooth, almost salamander-like lizard. Maybe they are already in the Tongue Range along Lake George, prime rattlesnake habitat, given that at least one guidebook suggests an outlier population in the uplands around Lake George?

Wet Salamanders and Dry Lizards

In the Adirondacks and Northern Appalachians, we are blessed with many salamanders — which are amphibians — but few or no lizards, which are reptiles. To oversimplify, we find salamanders commonly on our woods walks in spring because we are in a wet region. We most often see the florid red efts, terrestrial phase of the eastern newt, but if we're profoundly fortunate and observant, a dozen more species might let us see them. (See next chapter for more on salamanders.)

If we tread instead Southwest deserts and grasslands, we see a dazzling variety of lizards but few if any salamanders because there it is too dry for most amphibians.

Skink Link to our Dinosaur Forebears?

Some of you may already know the answers, but I am anxiously awaiting news on whether we already have skinks in our homeland, and if so, where they are and how we may help ensure they prosper here. Our local population of timber rattlesnakes — one of the northern-most outposts for this gentle, comely reptile — might tell us, if we listen carefully, how to live harmoniously with our region's one true lizard, a poignant affiliation with our dinosaur forebears of 70 million years ago.

If skinks come our way, they will need protected areas, like Split Rock Wild Forest, with plenty of rocky ground and down logs and leaf-litter for cover where they will quietly dart about feeding on insects.

Chapter 13:
Salamanders
Little Things that Run a Forest

*The salamanders we see dead on the roads by the scores every spring and summer are red efts,
the terrestrial phase of the eastern newt, vulnerable to road-kill, as so many amphibians and
reptiles are. © Larry Master, www.masterimages.org*

Be honest now. Have you ever squashed an eft? That is, have
you inadvertently run over the terrestrial, juvenile, bright-red form
of the eastern newt (*Notophthalmus viridescens*)? I know I am guilty,
probably several times over. Unless you have transcended the
American addiction to cars, you have probably crushed efts and
other amphibians during your travels. We can reduce chances of
that tragedy by slowing down and minimizing nighttime driving.

Efts are the salamanders we most often see trying to cross
roads in northern New York. Red-backed salamanders (*Plethodon*

cinereus) may be even more abundant in our forests, but unless you commonly overturn rocks and logs you seldom see them.

With complex life cycles involving both land and water, salamanders quietly amble and swim throughout our Adirondack forests and waterways. The typical human resident of Adirondack Park may only see a few salamander species in her lifetime, but – according to a field guide we all should consult, *The Amphibians and Reptiles of New York State*, by James Gibbs and fellow herpetologists – eighteen salamander species are native to New York, and at least half of these reach the northern part of our state.

Why Salamanders Matter

Along with salamanders' intrinsic value and beauty, these little creatures are important for preying on insects (especially mosquitoes, in the amphibians' and insects' respective aquatic larval forms), regulating soil nutrient and carbon flows, serving as prey for birds and other larger animals, and telling us how healthy the waterways and forests of our home are.

Simply speaking, abundant and diverse suites of salamanders indicate healthy lands and waters. Impoverished salamander populations mean habitat loss and degradation. Fortunately, our salamander populations in Adirondack Park are *relatively* healthy and diverse, as compared to those of more fragmented regions.

The great entomologist and conservation biologist E.O. Wilson thirty years ago wrote an essay for *Conservation Biology* about "The Little Things that Run the World." Wilson (author of *The Diversity of Life*, *Half-Earth*, and many other important books) showed in this article how small organisms we barely notice are immensely important to life on Earth. Indeed, Wilson reminded us, we humans would probably not long survive without the Little

Things that Run the World — though they, in contrast, might do better without us.

Conservation biology has lately been affirming that big creatures — especially keystone carnivores like wolf and cougar — are also tremendously important to natural checks and balances for maintaining biological diversity. Wilson's point stands though: We ignore or disparage tiny creatures, like bugs and slugs, at our own loss. In the northern forest of Adirondack Park and surrounds, salamanders are among those little creatures of outgrown importance.

Indeed, as forest ecologist Joan Maloof notes in her beautiful book *Nature's Temples: The Complex World of Old-Growth Forests*, salamanders may comprise much of the animal mass of a healthy mature forest — potentially outweighing all mammals and birds combined. Dr. Maloof also explains why salamanders fare best in old-growth forest, with abundant down logs and vernal pools and other moist microclimates.

Grandest of salamanders to extend its range into northern New York is the mudpuppy (*Necturus maculosus*), which may grow to a foot and half long. Mudpuppies, like their even bigger distant cousins hellbenders (whose range extends into southern New York), but unlike most salamanders, are fully aquatic. Mudpuppies inhabit streams, ponds, and lakes across much of New York, including the Champlain Valley, but apparently they do not reach the colder waters of the central Adirondacks. Despite mudpuppies' wide distribution, rare and lucky is the person who sees one.

Like many salamanders, mudpuppies eat a wide variety of smaller animals, including insects and mollusks. People sometimes kill mudpuppies intentionally under the mistaken impression that the salamanders are poisonous, or unintentionally with lampricide.

Dangers to Salamanders

Jefferson salamanders (*Ambystoma jeffersonianum*) live throughout forests of New York, but again, are not often seen by people. Part of a family known as "mole salamanders," after their larval aquatic phase, they live largely underground and may depend on burrows dug by small rodents. Like many semiaquatic and aquatic animals, mole salamanders are susceptible to acid rain – a problem that may worsen again, if political officials succeed in weakening clean air laws. Jefferson salamanders may hybridize with blue-spotted salamanders (*A. laterale*), also native in our region, yielding complex genomes that blur species boundaries (and hinting at pairings that make our social mores seem dull). You are more likely to see another cousin, the spotted salamander (*A. maculatum*), as brilliant yellow or orange spots on a black back trying to cross a wet road.

These mole salamanders are among the earlier of spring migrants, traveling to vernal pools and wetlands soon after snow and ice melt to find mates and breed. Vernal pools and wetlands are essential to salamanders' and frogs' wellbeing, for they are generally free of the fish that would otherwise eat the young amphibians. Where we don't protect wetlands – which we do, to varying degrees, in Adirondack Park – we lose much of our wildlife.

Other salamanders of our region include northern dusky and Allegheny Mountain dusky, northern two-lined, and spring salamanders. These modest-sized salamanders inhabit streams, springs, and seeps, as well as vernal pools and intact forests. They too may be lost from an area if it is heavily logged or wetlands drained or new roads built.

So please look closely if you must drive at night, especially on warm rainy nights in spring, when salamanders and frogs by the millions — but each one an individual with yearnings and families, just like you and me — may be migrating to breeding pools. Even if invisible to us most of the time, salamanders are helping keep our forest home healthy and diverse.

As amphibians, salamanders depend on both healthy forests and clean waters, and do best in protected areas like Split Rock Wild Forest. © Bill Amadon

Section 3:

Winged Ones

Osprey have rebounded in the Lake Champlain Basin, thanks to bird protection acts, clean water laws, and the banning of DDT. They are commonly seen perched high up in their big platform nests, or flying overhead to or from the lake, sometimes with a fish in their talons to feed their young. © Roderick MacIver Arts

Birds, bats, and insects are the three groups of animals who have taken to the skies, in feats of athletic process that leave us grounded mammals in envious awe. Marvelous though it is, flight is perhaps not so exceptional numerically as we suppose. Birds worldwide comprise nearly 10,000 species, and most of these fly; bats include more than 1,000 species, all mammals of flight; and large fractions of insect species (likely the most species-rich class of animals on Earth) are capable of flight during at least one stage of their metamorphic lives. (Many spiders also take to the air at times, but they balloon, with spun webs, rather than flying with wings. Spiders are in the same phylum, Arthropoda, as insects, but in a different class.)

So we will just glance up at a few of the more charismatic flying species of our area, saving discussions of others for later. As a forest rambler who aspires to be a good naturalist when I grow up, among my main goals for coming years are to learn the dragonflies (ultimate athletes!) and butterflies (ultimate beauties!) of our woods and waters. Meanwhile, I will share a few notes on songbirds, raptors, and bats.

Chapter 14:
Raptors of Our Region
Soaring Beauties

Hawks and other raptors help regulate rodent populations, and they have benefited from migratory bird protection laws as well as land conservation. © Sheri Amsel, www.exploringnature.org

Overlooking for now the lives of more distantly related birds of strong talons and hooked beaks, we touch here only upon accipiters, harriers, buteos, and eagles. All of these are birds of prey, and I will let ornithologists explain why they have put the seemingly similar osprey and falcons in different families. Owls are birds of prey, too (as are many of the world's 10,000 or so bird species, if you include in the definition of 'prey' small animals like insects), but we will not look at their families in this chapter. Intriguingly, with most raptors, females are larger than males.

Hawks of Our Home

We have here in the Northeast three accipiters: sharp-shinned hawk, coopers hawk, and northern goshawk. Sharpies and coopers, as birders affectionately call the two smaller species, prey largely on birds, often in forest but sometimes around birdfeeders or in wooded suburban parks. Northern goshawks are more discriminating about their surroundings, and they generally live in deep forest and hunt birds, squirrels, and snowshoe hares.

One of my finer sightings in Split Rock Wildway was happening upon a goshawk finishing off a squirrel, less than fifty feet from the Barn Rock Bay trail in Split Rock Wild Forest. I have also been lucky enough to face without harm the northern goshawk's notorious temper — a parent (I am unable to discern mother from father with hawks) swooped down on me and squawked loudly, when I advertently got too close to their nest, elsewhere in Split Rock Wild Forest. I have also been privileged to see goshawks in conifer forests out West. Goshawks fare best in large blocks of mature forest, so their presence in Split Rock Wildway assures us our conservation efforts are succeeding.

An inexperienced birder might mistake a northern harrier for a large accipiter because of the similarly long tail and slender appearance. Whereas accipiters catch prey during short quick chases, usually in forest, northern harriers (also called marsh hawks) hunt by coursing — flying low and slow over marshes and fields, looking side to side, to find rodents, waterfowl, frogs, or other manageable prey. Cleverly, if not compassionately, harriers are among several birds of prey known to occasionally kill their quarry by holding it under water.

Our region is graced also with four beauteous buteos — soaring hawks with broad tails and wings. We only see rough-legged hawks here in winter, when these huge birds come south from their Arctic breeding grounds for easier hunting of rodents in big open areas. Red-tailed hawks, nearly as large, may also be seen here in winter, though many of them migrate short or medium distances south after breeding season. Broad-winged hawks migrate in groups, or kettles, thousands of miles south to winter in northern South America. Red-shouldered hawks usually are short or mid-distance migrants.

None of these eight hawk species is thought to be imperiled in our region, though past clearing of forests likely diminished numbers of some, particularly northern goshawk and red-shouldered hawk. Before Rachel Carson's landmark book *Silent Spring* sounded the alarm, pesticides took a terrible toll on raptors – and could again, if environmental agencies loosen restrictions on such poisons.

The Grandest Raptors

Eagles could suffer gravely once more, if we allow a return to the toxic practices of the pre-EPA era. Bald eagles have recovered beautifully in our area. We thrill to see them soar over Lake Champlain, and we can periodically watch them raise a family on a huge nest in a tall pine along the Split Rock shoreline. We actually see bald eagles more in winter than in summer, as some of the many along the Richelieu River and farther north come south in winter to scavenge fish and hunt ducks along ice edges.

The golden sight among raptors for the Northeast is the golden eagle. Golden eagles long ago were more common in the Northeast, and reasons for their decline here are not well understood. Golden eagles are still fairly common over undeveloped parts of the West (I commonly see them soaring high over desert, grasslands, and mountains while I'm hiking out there), but they are only rarely seen in Adirondack Park and probably no longer breed here.

I wonder whether restoring to Adirondack Park its missing apex ground predators might somehow also help restore its diminished top avian predators. I have seen bald eagles on frozen Adirondack lakes scavenging carcasses of ailing deer taken by coyotes. Now I want to see golden eagles finishing an ungulate feast begun by wolves!

Bald eagles are a symbol not only for our nation, but also for the success of our nation's environmental protection laws, particularly the Endangered Species Act and Clean Water Act.
© Larry Master, www.masterimages.org

Chapter 15:
Songbirds

Bringing Color and Song to Northern Forests

Red-wing blackbirds and many other songbirds seasonally inhabit marshes and swamps, some of our richest ecosystems in Adirondack Park. © Sheri Amsel, www.exploringnature.org

By mid-spring, all of our songbirds have returned to Split Rock Wildway and surrounding fields and woodlands, many of them having spent the last six or seven months in Central or South America. Spring is not as colorful or musical as it was before Euro-Americans started clearing forests, however. Migratory songbirds are less bountiful than they were decades ago, for reasons not entirely understood but almost certainly including fragmentation of the forests here on their breeding grounds and in their Neotropical winter homes.

The diminishment of songbird populations, the *Silent Spring* Rachel Carson warned us about half a century ago, is a tragedy that our generation ought to reverse: through preserving and reconnecting wildlands, reducing pollution, and restoring apex predators.

If we look carefully around our homes in the eastern deciduous forest biome, we see the consequences of cutting apart natural habitats, consequences that weigh especially on forest-nesting songbirds. Some biologists call these "edge effects," and they include:

+ invasions by exotic species;

+ extermination of top carnivores like cougars and wolves, which eat or chase away smaller predators but do not trouble songbirds;

+ consequent proliferation of opportunistic predators, like house cats and skunks, which do prey on birds and their eggs;

+ colonization of forest edges by cowbirds, which are brood parasites (laying their eggs in nests of smaller birds);

+ disturbance by noisy machines, which may scare away birds trying to nest;

+ and altered microclimates (forest edges being susceptible to desiccation, fire, and wind-throw).

Songbirds' Merrier Mysteries

Happier, more natural mysteries continue to surround songbirds, though.

How do they migrate thousands of miles each spring and autumn between tropical rainforest and temperate deciduous forest? Present hypotheses credit birds' uncanny senses of direction, magnetism, and ability to navigate by the stars.

How do they fly so far so efficiently? We probably each burn more calories on an annual Champlain Area Trails Grand Hike of twelve miles than a warbler burns flying from the Adirondacks to Central America.

Where do they hide their nests? Many nest on leafy ground or in the forest understory, hence their vulnerability to opportunistic meso-predators, like raccoons and domestic cats.

What do they eat? Many dine primarily on insects, making them beneficial to us not only for their music but also for keeping "pest" populations in check.

And maybe the most vexing songbird mystery for birders: where is the maker of that avian melody? Whether it is an evolutionary adaptation on the birds' part or just our inferior hearing or both, songbirds are usually hard to locate after leaf-out in May, even when their songs are near and clear.

Split Rock Wildway Songbirds

Despite his bright plumage, the male blackburnian warbler is more often heard than seen, singing for mates and gleaning insects from the upper branches of pines and hemlocks.
© *Larry Master, www.masterimages.org*

My family so enjoys seeing and hearing songbirds that we are protecting our hundred acres of Adirondack forest as a wildlife sanctuary and as part of Split Rock Wildway, the wildlife corridor this book explores.

Rewards each spring include winter wrens bubbling out that most joyful of tiny birds' songs; scarlet tanagers flashing red between tall hardwoods and singing a blues-style robin's song; blackburnian warblers revealing spots of blaze orange and whistling high up in hemlocks and pines; rose-breasted grosbeaks warbling with a liquid clarity that allows us to spot their hot pink chests; and those master flutists, wood and hermit thrush and veery, sounding like the most sonorous solo vocalists you seldom see.

Please protect your forest, if you own land, and if you have cats that go outside, please get for them bright collars with loud bells, so birds will see or hear the cats before it is too late.

Chapters 16:
Bats

Canaries in the Iron Mine?

With their extraordinary echolocation system and rapid flight, bats are expert hunters of night-flying insects. They are also intelligent and gregarious mammals. © Sheri Amsel, www.exploringnature.org

The concept of ecological indicator species was foreshadowed long ago by using canaries — small tropical birds, sensitive to invisible gases that could kill miners — to warn the men if carbon monoxide levels were dangerously high. An expression some of us absent-mindedly use, "the canary in the coal mine," comes from that rather exploitive history of animal use.

Other small winged creatures, bats – Earth's only true fliers among mammals ("flying" squirrels of North America and Asia and "flying" lemurs of Asia actually being expert *gliders*) – may be inadvertently playing a similar role in modern society.

Bats in Adirondack Park, particularly, depend largely these days on artificial subterranean chambers for hibernacula, perhaps largely because many of their original winter homes were somehow usurped or destroyed by people. Before recent die-offs of bats, many thousands of several species gathered each winter in old mine shafts from the era of iron and graphite mining. These old mines function for bats much like caves do, deep enough to have constant temperatures and humidity levels. (For more background on bats, see the Fish & Wildlife Service's White-nose Syndrome website and Bat Conservation International's website and publications.)

Aliens Undermining Bat Populations

Tragically, about twelve years ago, a tourist inadvertently carried an alien fungus (likely on his or her shoes, after visiting a cave in Europe) into one of New York's natural but commercialized caves. Thus, evidence suggests, was white-nose syndrome (WNS) brought to the United States. Since its arrival in New York, it has spread like the plague through hibernating bat colonies across the East and Midwest. The alien fungus has precipitated a biological meltdown, affecting most hibernating bat species in the East, with effects cascading down the food web.

Because of this one barely visible invasive species of fungus, millions of bats have suffered lingering hunger and hypothermia and death. Populations have plummeted. Fortunately, individuals of some bat species are showing resistance, and researchers now think some populations may at least partially recover. For the northern long-eared bat, however, extinction is a dire possibility, as few individuals of that species show resistance to the pathogen. Its cousin the Indiana bat was already listed under the federal Endangered Species Act and is now in still more trouble.

A cold hard lesson from this ecological disaster is that global trade and travel mean moving species around in ways that can wreak havoc for our wild neighbors. Another difficult reminder is that some habitats are so sensitive and critical that we should just stay out of them — such as where bats or snakes or other species susceptible to human disturbance congregate to sleep away the winter.

All bats are highly mobile, and even the winter hibernators migrate at least short distances between summer and nursery roosts and winter homes. These movements, too, urge us to live with careful consideration for our wild neighbors. Giant wind turbines have been shown to harm migrating bats and birds (suggesting that energy production should be at residential and local scales, as well as being renewable). Bats will have a better chance of recovering from the scourge of white-nose syndrome if we protect large intact forests and free-flowing waterways, as we are doing relatively well — but not yet well enough — in New York's Adirondack Park

Bats in Our Park

What bat species grace our lovely Adirondack Park? Of Earth's thousand-plus bat species (second most species-rich mammal order after rodents), we have nine.

Eastern red bats (*Lasiurus borealis*), colorful and handsome, live throughout the East, and they are migratory and largely solitary, thus not thought to be susceptible to white-nose syndrome (which, again, hits bats in large congregations in winter hibernacula).

Equally comely cousins, hoary bats (*L. cinereus*) also migrate south rather than hibernating in caves in winter and thus may be safe from WNS for now. They can be recognized, for any person lucky enough to get a close look, by their large size and grizzled fur. Another migratory bat of our area, silver-haired (*Lasionycteris noctivagans*), enjoys similar good-looks and a relatively safe snow-bird lifestyle.

We are blessed also with four members of Earth's most widely distributed genus of bats, *Myotis*, which world-wide includes over a hundred species, living in most temperate and tropical ecosystems. The *Myotis* bats of our cool area live communal lifestyles that, alas, make them vulnerable to the alien disease white-nose syndrome. Little brown (*Myotis lucifiga*), eastern small-footed (*M. leibii*), northern long-eared (*M. septentrionalis*), and Indiana (*M. sodalis*) bats all traditionally hibernated in large congregations through winter in caves that maintained constant temperatures.

In the Adirondacks and some other mineral- or coal-rich areas, these bats in modern times discovered mines, and established large winter colonies in those cave-like environments. Since the arrival of WNS, the mines have not been safe for the hibernating bats. Even more than before, it is crucial for people to stay away from these mines (unless part of a research team), lest we further spread the deadly disease.

We also have two other bat species that hibernate communally in large numbers. Eastern pipistrelles (*Pipistrellus subflavus*) swarm in autumn, seeking mates before entering cave hibernacula, where they are susceptible to WNS. Big brown bats (*Eptesicus fuscus*; probably accounting for many of the bats you still see on Adirondack evenings) use caves or old buildings for hibernacula. Happily, big brown bats appear to be resistant to WNS and they are now our most common bat.

Big brown bats seem to be better surviving the exotic pathogen that has decimated many eastern bat populations, and still may commonly be seen in Adirondack Park. © Larry Master, www.masterimages.org

Coexisting with Bats

Coexisting peaceably with bats means avoiding use of pesticides and other toxic chemicals that bats may ingest through their insect prey or through water; minimizing artificial outdoor lighting, which disrupts natural movement patterns of insects and other wildlife; keeping major infrastructure out of natural habitats; and protecting old forests.

This last point needs more attention. As Joan Maloof shows in her book *Nature's Temples: The Complex World of Old-Growth Forests*, bats are among the many types of wildlife that tend to fare best in old-growth forests with big trees, partly because some bat species roost and nurse their young under the flaky bark of large ancient trees or in cavities of big snags.

We should value and protect bats for many reasons, from utilitarian to ecological to familial. For pure utility (from human perspectives), bats are great allies. They devour some of the insect species that we find vexing, including crop pests, and are telling indicators of overall environmental health. Ecologically, they play vital roles as predators of various insects and in some regions as pollinators of night-blooming flowers or as seed dispersers. Aesthetically, bats add beauty, wonder, and mystery to the evening woods and the night sky.

Then there is the matter of relatedness: modern taxonomy suggests that bats may be part of a super-order including flying lemurs, tree shrews, and primates. The primate order, of course, includes *Homo sapiens*. You are closer to bats than you think.

Section 4:

Finned Neighbors

Tales of BIG FISH
in Lake Champlain

Muskellunge

Sturgeon

Champlain Monster

Lake Champlain and its tributaries, including the Boquet River, which runs through Split Rock Wildway, are well endowed with fish species, most of them little known to people. Unfortunately, many of these fish are woefully reduced in numbers or health due to human-caused problems, including dams, pollution, exotic species, and past over-fishing. In similar ways, we have reduced populations of native mussels, some waterfowl, and aquatic mammals. Ignoring their beauty, we exterminated a rare freshwater population of harbor seals. Perhaps even more than we need to restore and "rewild" damaged lands in the East, we need to restore and rewild aquatic ecosystems, most of which are badly out of balance. To do so, we need to remove unneeded man-made dams on the tributaries and outlet of the lake, protect broad riparian buffers along these streams, otherwise reduce pollution running into the lake, stop exotic fish stocking programs, commence native species recovery programs, and prevent further introductions of exotic species. We need to take and spread great pride in the wild and growing beauty of Lake Champlain.

Chapter 17:
American Eels
Linking Deep Seas with Tall Mountains

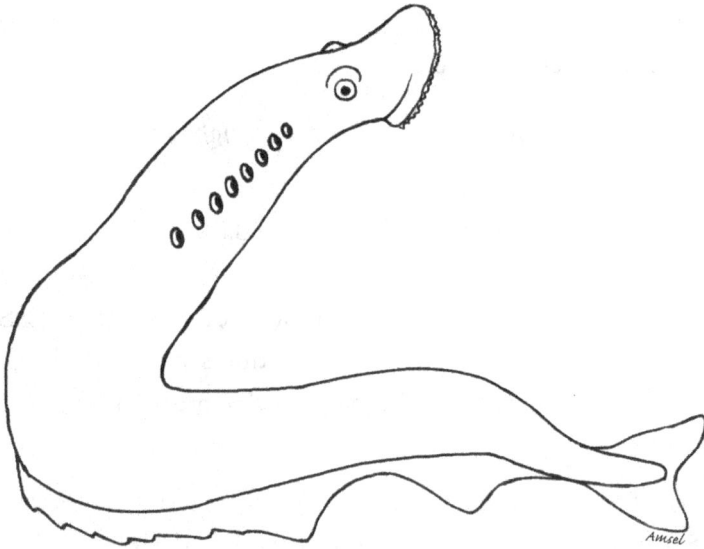

The diminishment of American eel populations may be a factor in the unnatural abundance of sea lamprey. Eel may have been a keystone predator of lamprey. © Sheri Amsel, www.exploringnature.org

Just as salmon are indicator and keystone species for the health of watersheds draining to the Pacific Ocean, American eels are indicators and keystones for Atlantic watersheds. American eels are native to most major freshwater systems from the St. Lawrence River (and even farther north) around to the Mississippi River (and even farther west).

American eels are part of an ancient family of fishes, the Anguillidae, which includes at least fifteen species. Most of these snake-like fish perform lengthy migrations to marine spawning habitats far from the streams where they make their livings – reminding us of the crucial ties between lands and waters.

Sadly, American eels are as diminished in eastern watersheds as are the several species of sea-going salmon in western ones. The Northeast was once blessed with abundant runs of eel – a prized food source for many native peoples – but now we have nearly forgotten they belong here.

Human Machinations Hurting Our Neighbors

Lake Champlain and its tributaries are some of the more upset ecosystems in our beloved Adirondack Park. As biologist Jerry Jenkins, author of the *Adirondack Atlas*, has wryly noted, implementation of the Forever Wild clause of the New York State Constitution, meant to protect the wildness and watersheds of New York's Adirondack and Catskill Parks, more or less stops at the waterline.

Most Adirondack lakes and rivers suffer repeated stocking of exotic fish; most Adirondack rivers have been dammed. Indeed, throughout the United States (with the welcome exception of Alaska), most major water bodies have been hydrologically altered and/or stocked with exotic species. We two-legged residents of the area have also hunted or fished some species to oblivion, reportedly including a freshwater population of harbor seals, present in Lake Champlain into historic times.

Dams may be the main culprit behind the diminishment of eel numbers in Lake Champlain and its rivers. Eels are diadromous, being born in the South Atlantic, migrating to and up streams to live much of their adulthoods in freshwater, then returning to the ocean to spawn. The young ones moving upstream can get over or around natural obstacles (such as small waterfalls), but man-made dams can be fatal. The St. Ours and Chambly dams built on

Lake Champlain's outlet, the Richelieu River, and dams built on rivers draining into Lake Champlain have hindered eel migration, though some of the barriers have been softened with fish ladders.

A Plea for American Eels

Why should we care about eels? First and foremost, they are native members of our regional biota, with their own reasons for being, quite apart from human utility. As well though, they may have been a keystone predator species in Lake Champlain, and their decimation may be part of the reason for the current unnatural abundance of sea lamprey — bane of Champlain sport fishers. Not that we should base conservation on economic arguments, but it is notable that experienced chefs will pay hefty sums for fresh eel flesh. It is a rich delicacy and could become a mainstay in revived fisheries in our region.

Restoring eels and other migratory aquatic species would mean removing obsolete dams or retrofitting them with fish passages; reducing pollution; discontinuing stocking of exotic species; protecting broad areas of riparian forest along and around water bodies; and regulating fisheries to favor native species. Our rewards will include the chance to see a wonder of the migratory world: a fish that might live many years in a small tributary of the Boquet River then make a heroic journey thousands of miles to spawn the next generation of eels somewhere out in the mysterious Sargasso Sea.

Chapter 18:
Sturgeon
Unsung Champs of Lake Champlain

Lake sturgeon still inhabit Lake Champlain, but are rarely seen. They are often deep in the lake naturally, but have been unnaturally diminished in numbers, partly through habitat destruction. © Larry Barns

Locals around Lake Champlain know well and joke often about the stories of Champ, a mythical monster of our deep-blue lake. Along with a bevy of fanciful explanations for Champ sightings (cousin to Scotland's Loch Ness Monster, among the most imaginative), one wild possibility is that the large humped back that various boaters have reported seeing on the surface of Lake Champlain is at least sometimes the dorsal fin of a lake sturgeon.

This should be thrilling enough, for sadly, lake sturgeon are vanishingly rare in our beloved but beleaguered lake. Icthyologists report that on the rare occasions when sturgeon are still seen or captured in Lake Champlain, they are old individuals, and that there is little if any evidence of ongoing breeding for these long-lived but slow-reproducing fish from the depths.

Reasons for the decline of lake sturgeon and several other big fish of Lake Champlain, including lake trout, landlocked Atlantic salmon, and American eel, are only partly known. Problems probably include the damages from dams on the rivers that drain into and out of Lake Champlain (including the outlet, the Richelieu River, which drains north to the Saint Lawrence, but has been fragmented by two dams); past overfishing of some popular "game" species; pollution; and the cascading effects from diminishment of certain other key species.

New York is blessed with three sturgeon species: lake, Atlantic, and short-nosed. Both the Atlantic and short-nosed sturgeons, like many members of the family Acipenseridae, live mostly in marine and/or brackish waters but swim up rivers every few years to spawn in fresh water. Before the damming of the Hudson River, these sturgeon may have ascended well into what is now Adirondack Park to spawn. As with nearly all of the two-dozen-plus sturgeon species in North America and Eurasia, they are threatened by habitat destruction, dams, pollution, and exploitation.

Lake sturgeon spawn in May or June in large rivers, on stone or sand shallows. Females mature at 14 to 26 years of age then spawn every 4 or 5 years. If protected, sturgeon live long and grow large. Reportedly, one individual lake sturgeon taken from south-central Canada's Lake of the Woods was 154 years old and weighed 208 pounds; another one from Lake Superior weighed 310.

Lake sturgeon prefer large water bodies and usually stay near the bottom, but occasionally breach vigorously, perhaps to keep groups together. (This might explain some reported Champ sightings.) They overwinter in deep, well-oxygenated water. They eat crustaceans, worms, insects, and mollusks – including zebra mussels. New York lists the lake sturgeon as Threatened; Vermont lists it as Endangered.

One line of speculation for the decline of some large fish suggests that sea lamprey are now unnaturally abundant in Lake Champlain because American eels may have been their major predators and eels have been drastically reduced due to dams in the Lake Champlain Basin, and in turn lamprey may now be harming large fish by parasitizing them.

In another possible trophic cascades story, I heard a biologist once wonder aloud if double-crested cormorants have grown overpopulated since harbor seals were eliminated from Lake Champlain. Seals would have hauled out on islands and islets of the lake, likely crushing cormorant nests and possibly even eating their eggs. Might the elimination of harbor seals have had reverberations throughout the lake adversely affecting some large fish populations?

Respecting Our Lake and River Neighbors

A theme of these wildlife accounts is peaceful coexistence with and greater appreciation of our wild neighbors. How can we learn to live benevolently with respect to aquatic species we never see and whose life cycles are poorly understood? We may not know enough to answer that question, but we can adopt a few general guidelines for supporting healthy natural communities in Lake Champlain and its tributaries.

Minimize pollution. Lake Champlain Committee has produced thorough reports on how to reduce phosphorous run-off and other pollutants in the lake. Among crucial steps are protecting broad forested riparian buffers along streams and shorelines; favoring organic farming practices; keeping livestock away from waterways; and preventing run-off from lawns and roads.

Avoid spreading invasive species. Here the culprits are sometimes motorboats or released baitfish and worms. Always check to make sure you do not have organic material on any boat or boot you are about to put into a wild water body.

Favor conservation and restoration of native fish and other aquatic species over "game fish" management. Fish and game departments all over the country have compromised the integrity of lakes and rivers by stocking fish that we humans like to catch. Fishing can be a sustainable as well as enjoyable way of hunting food — if it is managed not to augment introduced species but to restore native fish populations, including those champs of our biggest water body, lake sturgeon.

Chapter 19:
Rewilding Lake Champlain
Restore the Seals?!

Split Rock Wildway and Split Rock Wild Forest are named for this split in the rock, forming a small island in Lake Champlain. Some historians believe Split Rock served at times as the dividing line between different Native American tribes. © Larry Barns

Into historic times, reportedly, Lake Champlain harbored a freshwater population of harbor seals. The seals presumably colonized what would become Lake Champlain when it was a sea with a broader connection to the Atlantic Ocean. Our Euro-American forebears here in New York and Vermont apparently killed them off, in one of our many strikes at original inhabitants – including early human tribes – of our region.

The notion may seem far-fetched, in a society that has forgotten many of its original neighbors, but I humbly propose that we study the potential for reintroducing harbor seals to Lake Champlain.

Biological research might reveal that the seal here was too different from any remaining abundant populations for a translocation effort to succeed or be warranted. Earth does still have a few freshwater seal populations, including in at least one northern Quebec lake and in Lake Baikal, but maybe these are too far from Lake Champlain's past seals in time and place and genetics. Coastal populations of harbor seals, though, remain abundant in many places (off Cape Cod, for instance); so I hope we will not rule out the possibility of a restoration effort.

More feasible, perhaps, is restoring our populations of native big fish. Our lake should be teeming with landlocked Atlantic salmon, lake trout, American eels, lake sturgeon, and many other piscine predator species that are now sorely diminished.

We all rightly worry about land-use decisions in our area. Every year, though, we overlook commercial interests and government agencies making decisions that have life-or-death implications for many of the original inhabitants of Lake Champlain. We should collectively remove the obsolete dams, reduce the pollutants, restore the missing species, stop the exotic fish stocking, and halt the introduction of invasive species, before it is too late to have a healthy, clean, wild, and free Lake Champlain.

Metaphorically, at least, we need to *save the seals* to save the lake. Imagine the thrill of rowing past that little islet of rock in Whallons Bay (the one barely visible in high water, big enough to perch scores of gulls or cormorants in low water), once again a favorite seal haul-out. Your ears ring with the din of honking seals. Your skin is cooled by the splashes from seals launching into the water to scold you. An osprey races overhead to get past a watchful bald eagle who wants her hefty fish. A sturgeon breaches; a trout leaps... You smile and continue rowing out to

119

your favorite casting spot, where you just might catch a native salmon or trout big enough to feed your family tonight. Or to prepare for guests the eel you caught and smoked last spring.

Section 5:

Not So Easy Being Green

Thanks to the protection of much of the forest in Adirondack Park, and to a revival of small-scale organic farming in the Champlain Valley, our homeland provides abundant wildlife habitat and sequesters huge amounts of carbon, buffering against climate chaos.
© Bill Amadon

In his classic exploration of land ethics, *Sand County Almanac*, ecologist Aldo Leopold wrote that *the penalty of an ecological conscience is living alone in a world of wounds.* Those of us who have devoted our lives to exploring and helping protect wild places – learning to live with our wild neighbors – face daily, lonely anguish over humanity's insults to and assaults on wild Nature. The anguish is only worsened by realizing that we, too, are culpable for the losses of biodiversity caused by too many people consuming too many resources; that we are contributing to the extinction crisis.

Current trends in national politics make a dire situation even grimmer. Many elected officials are openly hostile to land conservation and seem dead-set on undoing our country's great legacy of establishing parks, refuges, and wilderness areas.

How, then, can one overcome despair and labor on to protect natural areas far and wide?

We may start by realizing how fortunate we are here in New York's Adirondack Park, where many of the land-use and wildlife population trends are positive. We may go on to learn about our wild neighbors and how to give them the space they need to thrive. We can support the land trusts and conservation advocacy groups who are helping protect wildlife habitat. Perhaps most difficult, we can make personal lifestyle changes that benefit our wild neighbors, such as:

- driving less often and less speedily,
- having small close families,
- getting our kids off their screens and out in the forest,
- letting our land grow wild, purchasing food from local organic predator-friendly farms,

- heating our homes with small-scale renewable energy (like firewood from a nearby woodlot),
- keeping our cats indoors or outfitting them with bright collars and loud bells (Birdsbesafe.com collars reportedly being especially effective),
- keeping our dogs from chasing wild animals,
- supporting conservation-minded candidates,
- running for local offices on an environmental platform,
- and choosing muscle-power over motor-power whenever possible.

Our beloved Adirondack Park is, arguably, the wildest landscape in the East, but it is not yet wild enough. It falls on our generation to finish rewilding it, so that it provides safe homes for all native species. The work may be hard, but the results can exceed our wildest dreams.

Chapter 20:
Natural Communities of West Champlain Hills
Our Special Homelands and Threats Thereto

Split Rock Wildway runs through the West Champlain Hills, which contain some of Adirondack Park's most biologically diverse ecosystems. © Kevin Raines

Most of us who live in New York's Adirondack Park are here because it is a beautiful, relatively wild and natural place. Winters are hard to endure (and getting harder, from some vantage points, as they become more erratic and less consistently cold) and jobs hard to find (and maybe also getting harder, as global overheating weakens the winter economy). Yet even those of us who love the Adirondacks may not realize how special is our own little part of it, here around the villages near Lake Champlain.

Our homeland in and around Essex and lakeside villages to north and south goes by various names or descriptors. Some folks know it simply as the *eastern Adirondacks, eastern Essex County,* or the *Champlain Valley*. With dark humor, some folks call our area the *Banana Belt of the Adirondacks;* so much milder are we than areas higher and farther into the Park (but even the direst climate models do not have us growing bananas this century!). More poetically, naturalist (and champion of heritage tourism) Gary Randorf dubbed our area the *Adirondack Coast*. More recently, another great naturalist and conservationist, Jerry Jenkins, has given our area the apt and redolent label *West Champlain Hills*, to encompass the modest but rocky hills just west of (and in a few places reaching through) Lake Champlain's west valley.

Split Rock Wildway: Critical Wildlife Corridor

Often in this book, I have promoted Split Rock Wildway as a vital wildlife corridor linking Lake Champlain with the High Peaks to the west. Split Rock Wildway is mostly within, and is one of the most intact parts of, the West Champlain Hills.

Split Rock Wildway comprises the wooded hills running from the Split Rock Range along Lake Champlain west over Coon Mountain then northwest over Boquet Mountain then west to the Jay Range. Split Rock Wildway also includes a swath of relatively intact habitat going southwest from the Split Rock Range past Westport then into the Westport Woods and on westward. Thus, if a wandering bear, heading west and up to cooler climes in summer, succeeds in crossing the barricade of I-87, she leaves the West Champlain Hills and enters the foothills of the High Peaks (which I sometimes think of as the "Wester Hills"). Split Rock Wildway, then, is a bifurcated, generally east-west running wildlife corridor including much of the roughly south-north running West Champlain Hills.

Botanical Significance of West Champlain Hills

I will resist repeating here my pleas for the wide-ranging animals that live in and travel through Split Rock Wildway. Instead, I will try to convince you to follow Jerry Jenkins's teachings on the botanical significance of your home territory. For Jerry has found, after decades of plant surveys across the Northeast, that we have one of the richest plant communities in the northern forest, right here in the hills we wander. The West Champlain Hills have an unusual plant community that Jerry sometimes calls the dry-rich oak-hickory-hophornbeam assemblage. Richness tends to go with lushness, so we are luckier than you might suppose, for having high species richness, including many species usually found farther south, in an ecosystem that is by Northeast standards remarkably dry (almost "xeric," to borrow a botany term that all Scrabble players should know).

Many of us complain about the number of rainy days here in the Adirondacks, but really, along Lake Champlain, we are relatively dry. We are in the rain shadow of the High Peaks, so we get much less precipitation than our headwater mountains. Plants need water, of course, but they also need nutrients, particularly calcium. Many of the hills west of Lake Champlain are blessed with surprisingly high levels of calcium in their soils, allowing "fertility indicators" (Jerry's evocative phrase) like fragrant sumac, woodland sunflower, rafinesque vibernum, douglas knotweed, a particular gooseberry or two, and white oak to prosper.

Other Aspects of the West Champlain Hills

Some of the thirty or so tree species in the West Champlain Hills are rare or absent elsewhere in Adirondack Park. Some tree species are near the northern end of their range here. © Sheri Amsel, www.exploringnature.org

I should not overplay our dry/rich aspects which tend to correspond to south- and east-facing slopes. We also have in the West Champlain Hills the more expected damp/rich sites, often in ravines where nutrients wash down and accumulate. In these fecund habitats look for maiden's-hair fern and a dazzling array of spring wildflowers. Our most famous example of this is the ravine through which runs the Adirondack Land Trust trail up Coon Mountain, which is fairly festooned with flowers each May.

We also have steep north-facing slopes that grow mostly eastern hemlock, mosses, and a small number of shade-tolerant herbs. What trees will fill hemlock's vital place if the dreaded invasive species hemlock wooly adelgid reaches our hills from vanguards in the Catskills or southern Green Mountains? Since American beech is also being decimated by an exotic species, and sugar maple is particularly susceptible to acid rain and over-browsing by deer, we cannot expect them to fill the role. Maybe birches.

Leaving aside those worries, the relative richness of our hills' soils is still something of a mystery. Jerry points out that the bedrocks in our area, including metanorthosite, are generally richer in nutrients than are most other country rocks of our region. New Hampshire granite, for instance, is more nutrient-challenged than Adirondack anorthosite. As well, Jerry has coyly hinted, the "plumbing" of our hills — the way water flows over rocks and percolates through soils — may tend to enrich some sites here more than happens in most of our region's uplands.

Indeed, Jerry has suggested (and is more fully disclosing in his *Northern Forest Atlas* series) that the West Champlain Hills may be botanically the richest area in Adirondack Park. For most of us, perhaps, this richness is to be celebrated more than it is to be investigated. Whatever the causes, we are fortunate to live in an area of great plant diversity, which may in turn enhance animal diversity. So the next time your teenage son or daughter asks, "Why do we live in this boring place?" you might answer that in fact we live in an extraordinarily rich and beautiful place, where richness is measured more in living beings than in ultimately worthless dollars.

Chapter 21:
Being a Good Neighbor at a Critical Time
Adirondack Life Melting, Mating, and Moving in Early Spring

Black bears are opportunistic omnivores, living largely on vegetation but occasionally hunting smaller animals or scavenging other predators' kills. © Larry Master, www.masterimages.org

Perhaps uncharitably, some of us lucky enough to inhabit Adirondack Park year-round refer to early spring as "Mud Season." Mud, slush, and soft ground surely are parts of the winter-to-spring transition here, but so are rushing rivers, running sap, surging freshets, budding trees, and migrating and reproducing animals.

Indeed, we could as well call this lustiest time of year "Mating Season" or "Movement Season." For throughout spring, most wild animals are searching for mates, food for their young, nest sites, or new territories. Movement is as central to wildlife as are food, air, water, and cover; yet it also brings risks — especially in a world fragmented by roads and other human development.

Let us recall a few examples of animals on the move in early spring: bobcats, mink, black bears, and other carnivores are traveling widely, to find food to meet the ravenous needs of their nursing young. Beavers old enough to yield their big brother and sister roles to the next generation are dispersing to find territories of their own. Early migratory birds, like red-wing blackbirds and mergansers and loons, are returning from their winter homes and reclaiming territories. Winter resident birds, like barred owls, may already have established nests and laid eggs, and thus will be hunting widely to feed their chicks. Frogs and salamanders are hopping and crawling to their breeding pools and swamps.

So, as upstanding members of the biotic community, it falls on us to be extra careful in our own travels during spring. If we drive our cars on a warm rainy night in early spring, we will likely run over a few of our neighbors. Alas, on such wet nights, we motorists kill countless salamanders and frogs as they follow ancestral travel routes, now dissected by roads, seeking vernal pools or other breeding sites. Even less able to sustain the tragic road-kill losses are the carnivores, raptors, and songbirds we too often hit, again especially in spring and at night.

There are long-term solutions to the tragedy of road-kill, including carefully placed tunnels under roads for amphibian crossings, modified culverts for fish passage, and overpasses for large mammal movement. As we build support for these engineering improvements — which can be made in concert with retrofitting infrastructure to make it more durable in the face of climate chaos — we should also make the personal changes that can help keep spring a season of motion. If we minimize nighttime driving and slow down, our wild neighbors can keep moving.

Chapter 22:
Roadkill Nation
Our Ongoing Avoidable National Tragedy

Countless millions of animals are killed on our nation's roads every year. Collisions between motorists and deer also account for about two hundred human deaths a year. © Sheri Amsel, www.exploringnature.org

In the summer of 2016, I again had the sad experience of coming upon a dead rattlesnake in the road while I was bicycling Lakeshore Road, next to Split Rock Wild Forest.

This was the third dead rattlesnake I have discovered on this road in recent years, added to the scores of dead porcupines and squirrels, and occasional dead beavers or foxes I find dead on roads fragmenting the eastern Adirondacks. I cycle roads through many otherwise mostly beautiful and natural parts of the country, East and West, and always I find, and mourn, road-kill. Sadly, we are a people that routinely runs over its neighbors.

Roads and the motor vehicles that drive them are major threats to wildlife at individual and species levels in most of the developed world, particularly the heavily roaded and driven United States. Roads block wildlife movement, and cars kill many of the animals that brave the perilous crossings. We Americans are complicit in the needless killing of billions of animals on roads every year. Some of this carnage – with victims ranging from snakes and salamanders to bobcats and bears to damselflies and dragonflies – is inevitable, so long as we get around primarily by driving, but much of it can be avoided.

How to Reduce Roadkill

Here are some basic measures we Americans could take to minimize the wildlife (and human) losses on roads:

1. Drive less often and less fast, especially at night when many animals are moving and are harder to see.

2. When you have a choice of routes, rather than driving small roads through wild places (like the aforementioned Lakeshore Road, which I have driven all too many times…), choose major roads through developed areas where wild animals are less common.

3. Help wildlife and transportation officials find where wild animals are trying to cross roads, and urge road departments to install safe wildlife crossings (overpasses or underpasses) in these places. When road engineers say the crossings are too expensive, point out that they save human as well as wild lives, and trot out statistics from Western Transportation Institute and other road ecology institutions on how wildlife crossings

more than pay for themselves, often in less than a decade, because of the savings of avoided collisions.

4. Urge wildlife and transportation officials to study culverts and replace old, unsafe, stream-fragmenting ones with new designs that are more durable in the face of worsening storms and more permeable to wildlife movement (especially for fish and amphibians).

5. Talk with your family, friends, neighbors, and town officials about how to reduce the tragedy of roadkill. Presently, sadly, from the standpoint of wildlife, we are the Roadkill Nation. We ought to live more considerately and generously than that.

Where in our region are safe wildlife crossings needed? There are many places where safe passage across roads would reduce wildlife mortality. I propose that we begin with:

* friendlier, more passable and durable culverts on rural roads through forested habitats;

* safe underpasses where Lakeshore Road and Route 22 go over streams in Split Rock Wildway;

* broader spans and more natural vegetation where I-87 goes over streams;

* and several wide overpasses across I-87 that can awaken motorists to road ecology even as they afford bears and bobcats and moose and other wide-ranging animals safe ways across the barrier.

A Post-Car Culture?

I believe in the long run that we Americans must reform our whole transportation system and urge other countries to do so as well. We must recognize that cheap oil will run out. We must convert to public transit and muscle-powered locomotion, live more locally, and burn much less energy. Sooner or later, rising fuel costs and destabilized climate will force us in these directions even if we currently lack the sense to embark on a more prudent, proactive path by ourselves. Yet even in the short term, without fundamentally altering our transportation system, we can take many sensible modest steps to reduce the tragedy of road-kill and the fracturing of landscapes.

Along with installing safe wildlife crossings – underpasses or overpasses – on busy roads, like NYS Route 22 and I-87, we can close unneeded roads in the backcountry, such as the long dirt roads that penetrate the Adirondack Forest Preserve, which will likely prove indefensible in the face of climate chaos anyway. Most important, we can *slow down*. Be ever aware that other creatures are trying to move about their daily lives, too, and that what for us may be travel-ways for them can be deadly roadblocks.

Chapter 23:
Wildways Forever
What Wildways and Rewilding Mean on the Ground

Conservation biologists suggest we must protect at least half the area of Earth's terrestrial and aquatic ecosystems to conserve most of biological diversity. Adirondack Park is more than half protected, but surrounding landscapes are much less than half protected. © Sheri Amsel, www.exploringnature.org

Wildways are wildlife corridors, broadly defined. They are how and where wide-ranging and dispersing animals, especially top carnivores, can find safe homes. The wolves trying to reclaim old habitats out West and in southeastern Canada, the wolverines somehow appearing hundreds of miles south of where the last ones were shot, the cougars braving dense networks of roads and guns as they move eastward from recolonizing outposts in the Black Hills and Badlands, the female moose who trekked from

New York's Adirondack Park to Ontrario's Algonquin Park — these are ambassadors of wildways and opportunities for people to relearn how to live generously with our original neighbors.

A term for these free-living creatures that my mentor Dave Foreman (author of *Rewilding North America* and other important conservation works) has revived from Middle English is 'wildeors' — literally, self-willed beasts. Ideally, we will make the world safe for wildeors again, such that they can wander freely far and wide, as they always did until we started persecuting predators and perceived competitors, wrecking their homelands, and precipitating an extinction crisis.

A story that powerfully captures the spirit of these wild wanderers is Will Stolzenburg's *Heart of a Lion*. In this carefully researched book, Will tells the account of a young male cougar, posthumously dubbed "Walker," who in 2009 left his natal territory in South Dakota's Black Hills, where state officials allow unsustainable numbers of the great cats to be shot every year. Walker successfully skirted busy roads, armed neighborhoods, barking dogs, and fearful people for thousands of meandering miles, trending ever eastward. Walker was documented by wildlife cameras at various places along his way in the U.S., with a long gap between Michigan's remarkably wild but cougar-deprived Upper Peninsula and northern New York's huge Adirondack Park, where he was seen in winter 2010-11. Most likely, Walker traversed southern Ontario during the many months he went undocumented. Likely, too, he returned to the U.S. via the Algonquin to Adirondack (A2A) wildlife corridor, maybe following a similar route, though opposite in direction, as had Alice the moose a decade earlier.

Ironically, Walker probably reached Adirondack Park (where one of my trusted outdoor friends thinks he saw the great cat, just miles from my cabin) about the time I was starting my 7,500-mile ramble through the wildest parts of the East, investigating how panthers might move north from Florida. Unfortunately, though he found good habitat and ample prey in the Adirondacks, Walker found no mate, so started moving again in the spring of 2011. Heading south and east, he may have reached the Atlantic Coast, before being tragically killed on the Meritt Parkway in Connecticut by a car he could not dodge: another bittersweet story of a young male looking for love in all the wild places, till finally falling victim to human machines.

About the time I learned of Walker's tragic end, I was trekking north through Florida's wildlands and learning of wide-wandering animals there. The story I remember most is of a young male black bear who left his home territory (as young male mammals seem wont to do) and headed north. Encouragingly, he survived his long foray, and followed closely the wildlife corridors that conservation biologists Reed Noss, Tom Hoctor, and others had identified and worked to protect across the state. This young bear made it as far north as Interstate 4, which bisects the state and fragments habitat southwest to northeast, from Tampa to Daytona. The bear could not safely get across that major barrier – which urgently needs more safe wildlife crossings – and returned south, roughly to his place of origin, after a walkabout of hundreds of miles fragmented by roads and other development but still loosely connected by wildlife corridors that conservationists have been desperately working to protect.

Rewilding and Wildways

The restoration of original habitats by top carnivores and other extirpated species is a health-renewing process captured in the poetic term 'rewilding' (coined more than twenty years ago by Dave Foreman, and further defined in 1998 in a classic *Wild Earth* article by Michael Soule and Reed Noss, called "Rewilding and Biodiversity: Complementary Goals for Continental Conservation"). The wild corridors these animals travel through are described evocatively as 'wildways.' Colleagues and I first applied the term 'wildway' to the Adirondack wildlife corridor we have been laboring for two decades to conserve, linking the Champlain Valley with the High Peaks. We named it 'Split Rock Wildway'; and since then, the term 'wildway' has spread.

For a quarter century, activists and biologists with Wildlands Network, The Rewilding Institute, and scores of regional conservation groups have been champions for a process and a vision that are biologically simple but socially complex. These conservation leaders advocate expanding existing protected areas – especially Wilderness Areas and National Parks on public lands – into large core reserves, reconnecting them via broad wildlife corridors, and reintroducing to them (or welcoming back in them) missing species, especially keystone animals like wolves, cougars, beavers, salmon, and eel. These advocates for wild Nature know what it would take to restore and protect North America's great natural heritage and indeed the rich dance of life throughout Earth, but gaining these protections on the ground and in the water and with respect to big toothy animals is proving socially complicated and politically difficult.

How Much Wilderness Is Enough?

To give an idea how much 'rewilding' we are talking about, consider that the esteemed conservation biologist EO Wilson has lately argued in his highly acclaimed book *Half Earth* for protecting at least 50% of Earth in ecological reserves. Earlier, Wildlands Network and Society for Conservation Biology cofounder Reed Noss had argued that to preserve the full range of biological diversity, we would need to fully protect a fourth to three-fourths of each natural ecosystem type and learn how to sustainably manage most of the rest.

Wilson has simplified this into his *Half Earth* goal: protect half of the total area of aquatic and terrestrial ecosystems in their natural state and use the rest much more sustainably than we heretofore have. Less than half for wild Nature virtually guarantees that the extinction crisis continues – already with a species extinction rate perhaps a thousand times the pre-human background rate, and accelerating quickly.

In North America, Wildlands Network and The Rewilding Institute have shown what a rewilded continent, or a Half Earth vision, would look like. These continental conservation groups and their many regional partners have argued for protecting broad wild swaths along the great mountain chains and across the great boreal forest – continental wildways. They have shown that other parts of a successful rewilding plan include:

* installing safe wildlife crossings on roads that fragment habitats;

* liberating rivers from obsolete dams;

* reintroducing or augmenting populations of missing or diminished species, especially the apex carnivores that are so central to ecosystem health;

- providing economic incentives for private landowners to steward their lands for wildlife;

- and generally expanding and reconnecting protected areas.

Biologically speaking, then, solutions to the extinction crisis are known. Socially speaking, though, solutions remain elusive. We know what needs to be done on the ground; we do not know how to convince people to make these steps feasible. Almost certainly, some of us believe, a prerequisite for achieving adequate continental reserve systems is admitting we humans are too many and those of us in wealthy nations consume too much. Until we peacefully, voluntarily, compassionately lower our own numbers, through universal access to education and family planning services, habitat destruction will continue and the extinction and climate crises will worsen.

Learning to Accept Others

The gap between biological understanding and social acceptance is partly because wildlife corridors are necessary but not sufficient. Coexistence is equally important, yet even that, which would not necessitate many changes on the ground, is proving difficult. As Dave Foreman wrote many years ago in *Wild Earth* magazine, support for conservation is a mile wide but only an inch deep. Most people from most countries probably would agree that we should collectively protect and restore the natural world. Most people in most countries do not, however, consume, vote, or otherwise live in accordance with Nature's needs.

How to make ourselves do so? How do we raise a generation of young people who live for a wild future, who choose to have small close families and leave plenty of space for wild neighbors? No one can wholly answer that question; many people can in small parts. Among the answers are surely the wild ambassadors making heroic journeys to old and new homes.

Natural ecosystems with a full range of native predators — from snakes to owls to foxes and beyond — are healthier for wildlife and for people who live nearby. © Sheri Amsel, www.exploringnature.org

Much can be said also about the two-legged champions for wildways. For every wide-wandering wildeor trying to reclaim old homelands, there is probably at least one team of fiercely dedicated, underfunded, overworked conservationists striving mightily to protect and reconnect their constituents' wild habitats. Books have been and will be written by and about these great wildlife defenders and wildways advocates (whose elite ranks include Henry David Thoreau, John Muir, Rosalie Edge, Rachel Carson, Marjorie Stoneman Douglas, Mardie and Olaus Murie, Jane Goodall, George Schaller, Paul Watson, Doug and Kris

Tompkins, and leaders of the Eastern and Western Wildways Networks).

The wildways champions who most inspire me, though, are the wildeors themselves — like Walker, that brave young male cougar who a few years ago may have slipped through Split Rock Wildway without any of us knowing it. All the animals who walk, trot, fly, or swim untold leagues to reclaim ancestral homelands are telling us, with their feet, their wings, their fins, how life should be. These wolves, cougars, lynx, bears, wolverines, fishers, moose, migratory birds, salmon, eels, whales, sea turtles, and kin are reminding us how to be better neighbors, how to *coexist*. These self-willed creatures are giving us wild hope for a better, more peaceful, richer Planet Earth, restored to natural beauty, with safe homes for everyone.

Acknowledgements

The author has noted before that (borrowing from a former New York senator), *it takes a community to save a corridor.* Applying that lesson to a tangible piece of ground – to Split Rock Wildway, the wildlife corridor that is the setting for these accounts – a whole human community of support will be required to complete protection of this vital link among natural communities of the Northeast.

We thank every group and individual in New York's Adirondack Park and beyond who has supported land conservation in this area. We thank especially the land trusts of this area: Northeast Wilderness Trust, Champlain Area Trails, Eddy Foundation, Adirondack Land Trust, Adirondack Nature Conservancy, Open Space Institute, and Lake Champlain Land Trust; the conservation advocacy groups who defend wild places, including Adirondack Council, Protect the Adirondacks, Adirondack Wild, and RESTORE: The North Woods; the continental conservation groups that inspire these wildways efforts, particularly Wildlands Network and The Rewilding Institute; the scientific and educational groups who inform conservation efforts, especially Keeping Track, Wildlife Conservation Society, Northern Forest Atlas Project, Algonquin to Adirondack Collaborative, Old-Growth Forest Network, Eastern Native Tree Society, Cougar Rewilding Foundation, and Wild Farm Alliance; the government agencies who (at their best) help protect land and wildlife, particularly the New York Department of Environmental Conservation, Adirondack Park Agency, and US Fish and Wildlife Service; and likewise the local government bodies and officials who sometimes (not always and never enough, but we anticipate ongoing improvement) support protection and restoration of land

and wildlife, most relevant here being officials in Westport, Essex, and surrounding towns. Special thanks go to Eddy Foundation for underwriting production costs of this book.

At least as many thanks are due the individuals who support these organizations, and others who may (without any particular affiliation) support wildlife conservation of their own accord. Helpful friends and family members are far too numerous to name here, but those without whom this little book would not have coalesced include wildlands philanthropists Jamie Phillips, George Davis and Susan Bacot-Davis, and the Klipper family; nature artists Bill Amadon, Sheri Amsel, Steven Kellogg, Rod MacIver, and Kevin Raines; photographers Larry Barns and Larry Master; Champlain Area Trails leaders Chris Maron and Matt Foley; and naturalists and biologists Mike DiNunzio, Brett Engstrom, Michale Glennon, Jerry Jenkins, Elizabeth Lee, Sue Morse, and Gary Randorf.

We stop there, lest our credits supplant our story. We leave out many this time; but we have not forgotten you, and we look forward to working with you long into the future, to keep our home safe for all creatures.

About the Artists

Bill Amadon spent the first 40 years of his life in Piseco in the southern Adirondacks. He worked as a campground faculty supervisor for the state of NY for 18 years before relocating to the Westport/Essex area. Bill has BFA from SUNY Plattsburgh, and as an artist developed an intense interest in portraying the wild lands of the region at early age. He has served on the board of the Adirondack Art Association and was once board chair. He is also an environmental activist with a focus on protecting the Adirondack Forest Preserve from degradation for any reason. Bill is currently on the staff at CATS (Champlain Area Trails), which conserves land and is building a community connecting trail system throughout the Champlain Valley region.

Sheri Amsel has written and illustrated more than 25 children's books and field guides. In 2009, she was awarded the *Elizabeth Abernathy Hull Award for Outstanding Contributions to the Environmental Education of Youths*, by the Garden Club of America. Her work has moved online with exploringnature.org, a comprehensive illustrated science resource website for students, educators and homeschool families. Sheri works out of her home studio in the Adirondacks.

Larry Barns has had a career as a corporate and editorial photographer in NYC, where he lived for many years. He has worked for numerous companies, hospitals, and business magazines, in the process photographing more than half the Chairman of the Fortune 500 companies. For the last 15 years he has worked with the artist/filmmaker Shirin Neshat. The photographs he takes for her are shown in major museums and galleries around the world. He also works on his own personal projects.

Steven Kellogg graduated from The Rhode Island School of Design fifty-five years ago, and after receiving a fellowship to study for a year in Italy, he began submitting stories and illustrations to publishers. Since then, he has published one hundred and twenty books, with a number of new projects now underway in his studio on the western shore of Lake Champlain.

Roderick MacIver is an artist and writer living near Essex, New York. Many of his books, such as *Art As A Way of Life* and *The Heron Dance Book of Love & Gratitude*, which celebrate the beauty and mystery of the natural world, can be found on Amazon. Hundreds of his paintings can be viewed on his website, roderick-maciver-arts.com.

Larry Master is a conservation biologist, a zoologist, and, in his retirement, a conservation photographer. He has been photographing wildlife and natural history subjects for more than 60 years. After doctoral and post-doctoral studies at the University of Michigan, Larry spent 20 years with The Nature Conservancy (TNC) and 6 years with NatureServe, most of that time as Chief Zoologist. In his retirement he serves on boards of NatureServe, the Adirondack Explorer, the Ausable River Association, Northern New York Audubon, and the Northern Forest Atlas Foundation, as well as on the Wildlife Conservation Society's Adirondack Advisory Group, the Science & Recovery Advisory Board of Living with Wolves, the Vermont Center for Ecostudies Science Advisory Council, and the American Society of Mammalogists' Mammal Images Library. Larry resides in Keene, New York.

Kevin Raines earned an MFA in Painting from Concordia University in Montreal in 1979 and returned to the States as a figurative artist, commission portrait painter, illustrator, and Professor of Art at Notre Dame of Maryland University. A New

York resident; he lives and works in Maryland and the Adirondacks. Drawing his inspiration from the beauty of the landscape and his passion for conservation, Raines has worked closely with local and international conservation science agencies for over 35 years to promote public awareness of our natural environment.

About the Author

John Davis is a wildways scout, editor, and writer. He co-founded Wildlands Network, a quarter century ago and works also with its sibling group, The Rewilding Institute. John makes his living partly through conservation field work, primarily within New York's Adirondack Park, where he lives.

In 2011, John completed TrekEast, a 7,600-mile muscle-powered exploration of wilder parts of the eastern United States and southeastern Canada. This nine-month long journey, sponsored by Wildlands Network and following lines suggested in Dave Foreman's book *Rewilding North America*, promoted restoration and protection of an Eastern Wildway. In 2012, John reflected on that adventure in *Big, Wild, and Connected*, published by Island Press.

In 2013, John headed west to undertake another epic trek. Starting in Sonora, Mexico, and traversing the Spine of the Continent as far north as southern British Columbia, Canada,

TrekWest ground tested mapped wildlife corridors while promoting large-scale habitat connections, big wild cores, and wide-ranging species, including apex predators—all of which would be well served by fuller protection of the Western Wildway. This conclusion and other observations from John's adventure are documented in, *Born to Rewild: Trekking the Western Wildway*, an hour-long film released in 2017.

John Davis serves on boards of The Rewilding Institute, RESTORE: The North Woods, Eddy Foundation, Champlain Area Trails, and the Cougar Rewilding Foundation. John co-founded the *Wild Earth* journal and served as editor from 1991 to 1996, when he went to work for the Foundation for Deep Ecology, overseeing their Biodiversity and Wildness grants program from 1997-2002. He then joined the Eddy Foundation as a board member and continues to serve as volunteer land steward for that foundation in its work to conserve lands in Split Rock Wildway. This wildlife corridor links New York's Champlain Valley with the Adirondack High Peaks via the West Champlain Hills, as explored in this book. John served as conservation director of the Adirondack Council from 2005 to 2010.

Resources for Split Rock Wildway and Beyond

Specific websites and contact information are subject to change and easily found on Google, so are not provided here. This list is far from complete, and I apologize for the many institutions and publications overlooked.

Local

Champlain Area Trails – maintains trails and saves land in Adirondack Champlain Valley

Eddy Foundation – saves land and supports green economy in Split Rock Wildway (and also has conservation projects in southern California and Dominican Republic)

Boquet River Association and AuSable River Association – work for health of Boquet and AuSable Rivers and tributaries and watersheds

EssexonLakeChamplain.com – website with community news for Essex, NY area

Essex Editions – publisher of this and other books important to life on the Adirondack Coast

Westport Hotel – comfortable place to stay and eat, while exploring eastern Adirondacks

Essex Inn – fine lodging and dining in historic Essex village, north of Split Rock

Ledge Hill Brewery – micro-brewery near Westport train station

Dogwood Bakery – popular eatery between Westport and Essex on Route 22, good destination for lunch after hike on nearby CATS trails

Depot Theatre – conveniently located at Westport train station (Amtrak service from New York City to Montreal) and hosting excellent plays throughout summer

Leep-Off Cycles – bike repair and sales shop in Keene Valley, NY, and source for biking ideas

Solace Bicycles – custom-made bikes, designed in Westport, and general purveyor of adventure bicycling

Regional

Northeast Wilderness Trust – keeps land Forever Wild wherever possible in Northeast US, key land trust in Split Rock Wildway

Adirondack Land Trust – protects Coon Mountain, affording some of Split Rock Wildway's best views and richest plant communities, and other lands in Park

Adirondack Nature Conservancy – protects land and enhances habitat connections throughout Park

Open Space Institute – quiet but effective land trust with projects in Split Rock Wildway and far beyond

Lake Champlain Land Trust – mostly active on Vermont side, but now helping save land on New York side, too

Adirondack Council – powerful advocacy group pushing for Adirondack land protection and clean air and water

Protect the Adirondacks – holding the Blue Line to keep Forest Preserve lands Forever Wild and limit harmful development on private lands

Adirondack Wild – also fighting effectively for expanded Forest Preserve and smarter development of private lands

Adirondack Mountain Club – promotes and maintains trails and helps expand Forest Preserve

Adirondack Wildlife Rehabilitation Center – rescues wounded wildlife and educates visitors to its care facilities in Wilmington on coexistence with our wild neighbors

Adirondack Center for Loon Conservation – research and education for loons in Adirondack Park and beyond, with a visitor center in Saranac Lake

Northeast Wolf Coalition – network of groups educating residents on values of Wolves and other top carnivores

Lake Champlain Committee – environmental group dedicated to a clean natural lake

Bark Eater Trails Alliance – BETA is the leading voice for carefully placed mountain bike trails in Adirondack Park

Adirondack Explorer – comprehensive news & views on Adirondack Park exploration, recreation, culture, and politics

Adirondack Almanac – on-line daily news from throughout Adirondacks

LocalAdk – photogenic magazine on life and adventure in Adirondack Park

EmBark – outings journal, available through many Adirondack establishments

Northern Forest Atlas Project – superb field guides, plant charts, and websites crafted by biologist Jerry Jenkins & team in concert with Wildlife Conservation Society

Adirondack Atlas, by Jerry Jenkins – facts from biological to historic to demographic, on Adirondack Park, published by WCS's Adirondack Conservation and Community Program

Adirondack Wild Guide, by Mike DiNunzio and Anne Lacy — classic work on natural history of Adirondack Park, published by Adirondack Council

Wandering Home, by Bill McKibben — Bill's journey from his Vermont home to his Adirondack home, on which I had the privilege of guiding this environmental hero through Split Rock Wildway

Adirondack Park: Wild Island of Hope, by Gary Randorf — beautiful words and images of a successful but unfinished conservation story

The Dirty Life: On Farming, Food and Love, by Kristen Kimball — eloquent accounts of the challenges of farming in the Champlain Valley by the co-founder of the largest CSA in our area

Continental and Global

Wildlands Network — works especially in proposed Eastern and Western Wildways to reconnect wild places and restore missing species, including top carnivores

The Rewilding Intitute — resources for rewilding Earth

Cougar Rewilding Foundation — volunteer group dedicated to education and advocacy for North America's greatest cat

Project Coyote — education and advocacy group helping people all over the country learn to live with Coyotes and other carnivores

Wolf Conservation Center — fosters concern for Wolves and other carnivores with its captive breeding programs in Salem, NY, and its Ambassador Wolf programs for schools

WildFutures — a project of Earth Island Institute devoted to coexistence with wildlife, especially top carnivores

Wildlife Conservation Society — runs wildlife research and conservation programs world-wide and has program here in Adirondack Park that publishes reports on West Champlain Hills plant communities, Coexistence with Wildlife, the effects of Exurban Sprawl, Boreal Bird and Moose conservation and more

Center for Biological Diversity — touch legal-defense group for wildlife across our hemisphere

Island Press — publisher of hundreds of important books on environmental and conservation subjects, including several of those listed here

350.org — network leading charge for climate stability and justice world-wide

Rewilding North America, by Dave Foreman — prescriptions and visions of how to reconnect wild habitats and restore North America's great natural heritage

Man Swarm: How Overpopulation is Killing the Wild World, by Dave Foreman — a frank look at the fundamental problem no one wants to discuss—how our booming numbers are precipitating an extinction crisis

Saving Nature's Legacy, by Reed Noss and Allen Cooperrider — the fundamentals on why and how to save wild Nature

Continental Conservation, edited by Michael Soule and John Terborgh —conservation biology papers on why protecting Nature at larger scales is necessary

The Wolf's Tooth, by Cristina Eisenberg — trophic cascades and the importance of top carnivores lucidly explained

Where the Wild Things Were, by Will Stolzenberg — compelling discussion of why big wild animals and important and why overcoming irrational fears of them is difficult

Heart of a Lion, by Will Stolzenberg – poignant true story of one heroic Cougar's journey eastward half-way across North America

Cougar: Ecology and Conservation, edited by Maurice Hornocker and Sharon Negri – basic text on natural history and status of *Puma concolor*

Monster of God, by David Quammen – enthralling studies of big scary animals and our volatile relations with them

Nature's Temples: The Complex World of Old-Growth Forests, by Joan Maloof – scientific but clear look at the amazing diversity of original and ancient forests

Eastern Old-Growth Forests: Prospects for Rediscovery and Recovery, edited by Mary Byrd Davis – my mother's collection of papers on the ecological importance of old-growth forest and where it can still be found in East

Big, Wild, and Connected: Scouting an Eastern Wildway from Florida to Quebec, by John Davis – my account of TrekEast, a 7600 mile exploration of proposed Eastern Wildway

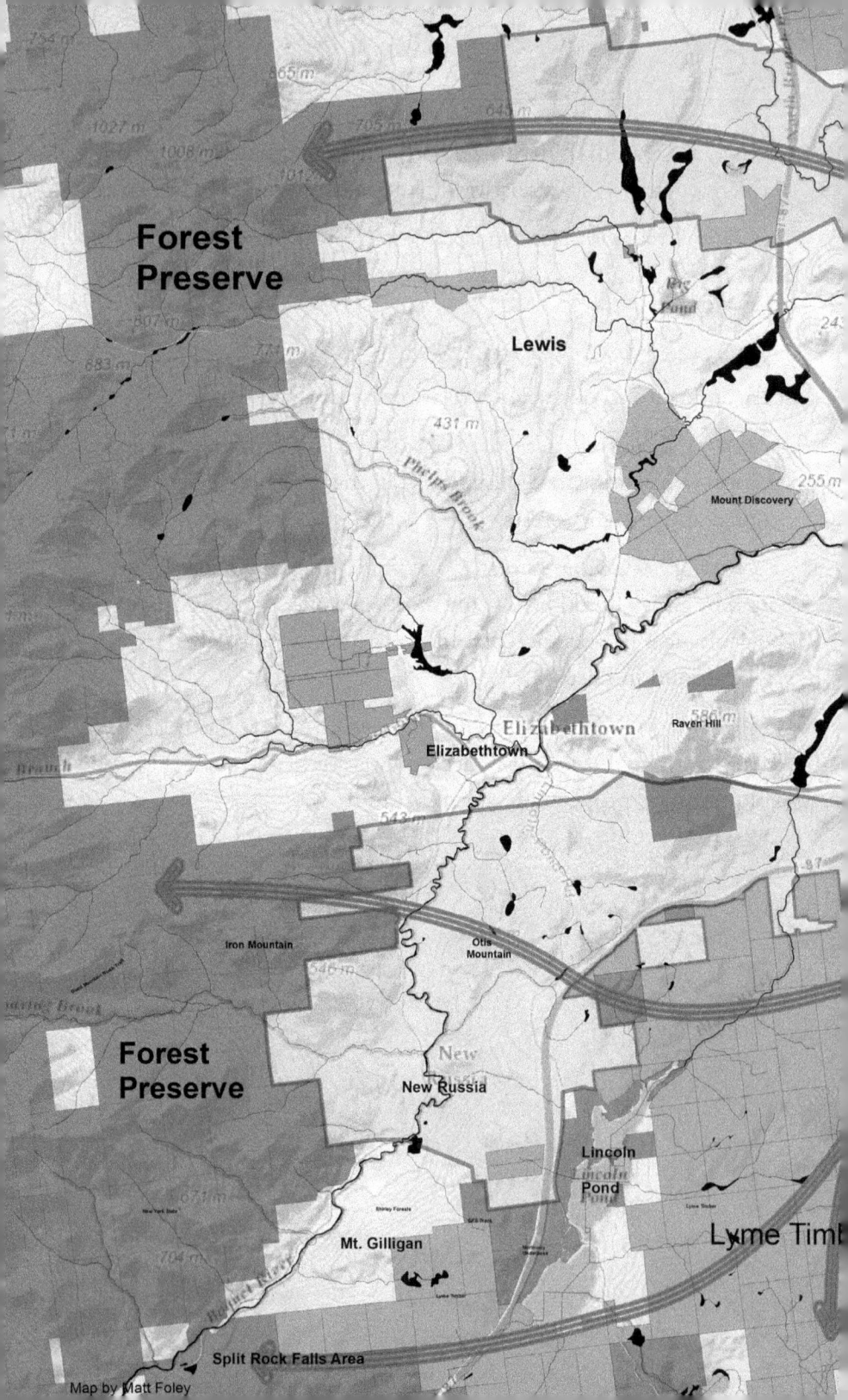

Forest
Preserve

Lewis

Mount Discovery

Elizabethtown

Elizabethtown

Raven Hill

Iron Mountain

Otis
Mountain

Forest
Preserve

New Russia

Lincoln
Pond

Lincoln
Pond

Lyme Timb

Mt. Gilligan

Split Rock Falls Area

Split Rock Wildway

Split Rock Wildway

Essex

North Boquet Mountain

South Boquet Mountain

Whallonsburgh

Split Rock Wild Forest

Coon Mountain

Wadhams

Westport

Kingsland State Park

Fields Bay

NEW YORK

VERMONT

Button Bay State Park

Button Bay

Otter Creek

Panton Rd

Dead Creek

www.ingramcontent.com/pod-product-compliance
Lightning Source LLC
Chambersburg PA
CBHW062057270326
41931CB00013B/3111